I0061178

THE SONG OF THE SOUL

The Transpersonal Dimension of Psyche and Sound

Lena Måndotter

Zurich Lecture Series in Analytical Psychology

ISAPZURICH

Volume 11

CHIRON PUBLICATIONS • ASHEVILLE, NORTH CAROLINA

"He shall cover thee with his feathers, and under his wings shalt thou trust: His truth shall be thy shield..."[1]

www.ChironPublications.com

Interior and cover design by Danijela Mijailovic
Printed primarily in the United States of America.

© Photograph front cover: Lena Måndotter
Cymatic sound figures and tortoise (page 41) from Water Sound Images
by Alexander Lauterwasser.
© 2006 MACROmedia Publishing. All Rights Reserved. www.cymaticsource.com

ISBN 978-1-68503-230-2 paperback
ISBN 978-1-68503-231-9 hardcover
ISBN 978-1-68503-232-6 electronic
ISBN 978-1-68503-233-3 limited edition paperback
ISBN 978-1-68503-504-4 limited edition hardcover

Library of Congress Cataloging-in-Publication Data

Names: Måndotter, Lena, author.

Title: The song of the soul : the transpersonal dimension of psyche and sound / Lena Måndotter.

Description: Asheville, North Carolina : Chiron Publications, 2024. | Series: Zurich Lecture Series in Analytical Psychology ; Volume 11 | Includes bibliographical references and index. | Summary: "At the core we are all vibrations, musical compositions in motion, and that is why we resonate in communion with the world of music. The human voice is the only instrument that sounds from within, and our singing voice is deeply connected to heart and soul. In the timbre and tonal nuances of the voice we can perceive subtle soul messages - way beyond words. The sound of the voice mirrors the movements in the depths of psyche, and this touches us profoundly. To liberate the voice is to liberate psyche. To free the sound is to free the soul. Singing requires deep listening, instinctual attention, pure vocal presence, and the song is a musical alchemical vessel for psychospiritual transformation. Music is a magical magnet, a sacred gift from the Muses, so that our songs may sound the mana of the Mysterion. Lena Måndotter's lifelong voyage with soul and song can inspire us all to reclaim our instinctual singing voice. C.G. Jung wrote that "music should be an essential part of every analysis." This book shows why and is a testament to the healing power of song"— Provided by publisher.

Identifiers: LCCN 2024038694 (print) | LCCN 2024038695 (ebook) | ISBN 9781685032333 (paperback) | ISBN 9781685035044 (hardback) | ISBN 9781685032326 (ebook)

Subjects: LCSH: Music—Psychological aspects. | Singing—Psychological aspects. | Music and mythology. | Music thaerapy.

Classification: LCC ML3830 .M17 2024 (print) | LCC ML3830 (ebook) | DDC 781.1/1—dc23/eng/20241023

LC record available at https://lccn.loc.gov/2024038694

LC ebook record available at https://lccn.loc.gov/2024038695

PRAISE FOR
THE SONG OF THE SOUL

Lena Måndotter's *Song of the Soul* is characterized by the fact that, on the one hand, it is drawn from her personal experience as a singer, song-therapist and Jungian psychoanalyst and is thus touching and convincing, and that, on the other hand, it draws on a great deal of mythological amplification material and relevant literature, thus anchoring the subject in the larger whole of an archetypal reality and a scientific dialogue.

The book is, as it were, a symphonic poem about sound and song as a numinous experience of the reality of the soul. The various mythological aspects that resonate in song are discussed in a broad arc. Hermes, Orpheus, the angels, the serpent. Music connects in both directions: upwards and downwards. Into the realm of the air and the spirit and into the realm of the earth and the underworld and the instincts.

Thanks to their transpersonal dimension, song and sound can lead us into a realm that can expand the ego trapped in its rational perspective and anchor it both in its instinctual level and in the open horizon of archetypal experience.

This richly documented book, which is full of fascinating insight, allows the reader to recognize in musical serpentines the astonishing dimensions of depth, mystery and soul that are inherent in sound and song. It will be of great use to vocal therapists, music therapists and singers, but also to lovers of sound and psychoanalysts in general who like and are able to listen.

Paul Brutsche
Ph.D. Jungian psychoanalyst, training/supervising analyst at ISAPZURICH.
Author of *Creativity: Patterns of Creative Imagination as Seen Through Art*

Lena Måndotter's *Song of the Soul* renews and deepens my vision of art healing. The ability of vocal expression to immediately access the range of emotion from the atavistic wilds, and the resulting fear of their power, to the most tender vibrations, and joyous play, requires the skill and care demonstrated in this book when working with others. The expressions are, in my experience, best released, and lovingly held, within the sacred spaces and world traditions presented here, all affirming Soul's ability to heal itself with song.

Shaun McNiff
Artist and University Professor Emeritus.
Author of *Art as Medicine, Art Heals, Integrating the Arts in Therapy, Trust the Process: An Artist's Guide to Letting Go* and *Imagination in Action: Secrets for Unleashing Creative Expression*

Whiskey in hand. Seat laid back. Lectures done. Flying home, watching Willie Nelson in *Honeysuckle Rose*. Strangely, I hear other voices singing, old-time country voices I recognize as Hank Williams, Bob Wills, Roy Acuff, and others. I begin to cry, sob uncontrollably. Passengers concerned; stewardesses wanting to know if I want a doctor. Finally, I calmed down. Later, I told my parents about this. My dad said he knew what I was experiencing. During my first year, he would rock me in his arms, singing out loud to country music radio of the late 30's: to cure his stuttering. It worked. Something I had never known about.

As I read Lena Måndotter's *The Song of the Soul,* my experience of those country voices came alive in ways they had not before; I knew what she meant by *soulsong.* Every page resonated with the myriad implications of my experience and brought forth not only the depth but the breadth of songs I had heard before I was one year old, before language, before conscious memory, and came back to me at 42 with sobs and tears.

Lena writes in words about something beyond the reach of words. But her experience in singing and song therapy made her words lyrical, and something came through. I found myself *humming* as I read–a new experience for me. As I read, the sense of mystery deepened. But Lena made it clear that soulsong as mystery was not to be subjected to the usual rational and linear tools of understanding. Mystery was a *guide* from the depths of the archetypal world. As Giles Quispel said, "Mystery is not to be solved, resolved, or dissolved. Mystery is to be embraced, loved, and out of that will come one's deepest sense of life, meaning, and purpose." This is the spirit and soul of Lena's book throughout, an ever-deepening revelation of this deepest secret. Get this book and let it sing to you and prompt soulsong from your depths. This is the gift of this book and of Lena's immersion in the mystery of soulsong.

Russell A Lockhart
Ph.D. Jungian psychoanalyst.
Author of *Psyche Speaks – a Jungian Approach to Self and World* and *Words as Eggs – Psyche in Language and Clinic* and *Dreams, Bones & the Future*

In this extensive study Lena Måndotter explores the archetypal aspects of the singing voice as the inner instrument that connects the soul and the heart. As a long-time inhabitant of Greece, she is at home with the country's myths and teases out Hermes' and the Serpent's capacity to connect with song. The book beautifully explores the direct expression of emotions carried by singing and suggests that this is of a different order to that conveyed by words. Måndotter makes the case for a place for music in the centre of an analysis. It is a book to be appreciated by all who want to explore the ways in which sound and singing carry and transmit emotions in their own unique way.

Juliet Miller
Jungian Analyst and Documentary Filmmaker.
Author of *The Creative Feminine and her Discontents – Psychotherapy, Art and Destruction* and *Art, Memoir and Jung: Personal and Psychological Encounters*

In *The Song of the Soul*, Lena Måndotter offers a moving testimony to the essential and numinous relationship between soul, sound, music, and the transpersonal. Drawing from her broad experience as a singer, song-therapist, and Jungian psychoanalyst, this volume integrates Måndotter's personal musical journey with archetypal themes, neuroscience, somatic experience, reflections on contemporary culture, the poetry of lyrics, and experiences from her consulting room. *The Song of the Soul* creates a rich tapestry that opens the reader's ears, eyes, and soul to the power of music to engage with psyche at great depth.

Mark Winborn
Ph.D. – Jungian Psychoanalyst, Clinical Psychologist and Musician.
Author of *Deep Blues: Human Soundscapes for the Archetypal Journey* **and** *Interpretation in Jungian Analysis: Art and Technique*

As a singer, musician, and music-therapist, I feel that Lena Måndotter's *Song of the Soul* is a musical soul journey into the mystical, symbolic, and archetypal worlds. We, who live in the world of sound, know how hard it is to translate this sounding world into words, but Lena has paradoxically managed to verbalize this non-verbal dimension.

For many years, in group courses and supervision, I have experienced Lena's skillful ability to navigate and therapeutically guide this song-therapeutic process where we are called to reclaim our holy soul voices. Her book is a musical testament to this knowledge, and she appears on the horizon as a messenger for the soul-song of humanity.

This book is very important for our times. It tenderly cares for *Song and Soul*, and it is a numinous recall to remember who we soulfully are as musical beings. Lena has woven a poetical tapestry of what the healing power of singing and music is truly - and finally about.

Marit Eneström
Singer. Guitarist. Pianist.
Music-therapist. Eurythmics- and Song-teacher: "Voice and Body" sessions and courses and at the Royal College of Music in Stockholm, Sweden

With *The Song of the Soul* Lena Måndotter presents a profound and very enriching study of the importance of music in therapy, based on her many years of work with Jungian song therapy. A central sentence of C.G. Jung, to which all statements in Måndotter´s work can ultimately be traced back, is: "*I feel that from now on music should be an essential part of every analysis.*

Music reaches the deep archetypal material that we can only sometimes reach in our analytical work with patients."

When you read this book, you get the impression, that you can no longer carry out therapy without using song and music, so inspiring are Måndotter's thoughts and experiences. She goes a long way by delving deeply into the archetypal history of music using a variety of mythological and spiritual references. Actually, no therapy should be without music, because singing means to use our soul-voice. From an early age, even from the time in the womb, song, tone, and music are deeply anchored in our souls, even in our genes as a primal language.

Måndotter, herself, is deeply present in her words through her own living experience. She is almost permeable to her thoughts and experiences and is therefore able to reach the reader´s psyche. Every one of us psychological therapists, but also music therapists, and indeed everyone interested in the soul and the effects of music, should read this book and be inspired by her wonderful and convincing statements. If you have not any experience with singing and music in therapy, her song-therapeutic work makes you curious to try out. The value and importance of the analyst´s or therapist´s soul-voice as an instrument for the patient´s healing psychological process is made aware – indelibly.

Irene Berkenbusch-Erbe
Ph.D. Jungian psychoanalyst, training/supervising analyst at ISAPZURICH

Lena Måndotter's *The Song of the Soul* is nothing other than just that, a soul song and a song for our collective soul. A scholar and multi-talented artist, this book is Måndotter's crown jewel in her diadem of life work. Herein she has harvested her knowledge and experience into a penultimate offering, bringing her soul to the souls of others with song, with words, myth, therapeutic practice, and with the sparking forces and fires of alchemical creativity. That we may all emerge from these pages singing.

Lisa L Lindsay
Ph.D. Clinical Psychologist. Leader of Jungian Somatic Workshops.
Author of *Arlo's Garden* and protagonist of *Avenge a Friend* – a Book
and a Documentary Film about a Deep Friendship with a Horse

I have known Lena Måndotter for many years and followed her career at a distance. I have listened to many of her concerts, and I have also participated in her experiential seminars and workshops *The Song of the Soul*. I have been overwhelmed and awed at her ability to guide her students to the deepest parts of their singing souls with a combination of encouragement, firmness, kindness, and a profound knowledge of what she is doing. In this book she describes in a fascinating way how she has obtained this unique ability and what insights and experiences she has gathered along the way. I sincerely love and admire her book, her song-therapeutic work and her moving singing and lovely songs.

Karin Hedner
MD Ph.D., and Leader of Ritual Dancing
Author of Rituell Dans – Livets Dans (Ritual Dance – the Dance of Life) and Undran och Förundran – Tankar om Livet (Wonder and Wonderment – Reflections on Life)

With *The Song of the Soul* Lena Måndotter shows how it is possible for us to "feel" the soul within the body, and how, via the expression of music or song, it is possible for deep movement within. As a singer, song-therapist and Jungian psychoanalyst, Lena has a wonderful gift to share with us.

In her book she uses amplification from Greek mythology, Jungian wisdom, and the symbolism of animals to reach our inner "hearing" and maybe also "conscious understanding." But most touching of all is to actually hear these songs and music, especially when sung or played with deep feeling from within. We are provided with a heartwarming experience via this book, and encouragement to allow and enjoy this deep expression of feeling and being who we truly are.

Sandy Schnekenburger
Adv. Dipl. (PSW), Jungian psychoanalyst and training/supervising analyst at ISAPZURICH

ENDNOTES

[1] Psalm 91:4, The Holy Bible, King James Version.

South of the sun
west of the wind
where the soulsong sings
and the spirit sounds
across the holy waters

FOREWORD
by Murray Stein

I grew up with Beethoven's opera, "Fidelio." My father, it seemed, had discovered his soul image (anima) in Leonora, the dramatic heroine. Disguised as a man, she liberates her beloved husband, Florestan, who has been unjustly locked away as a political prisoner in a dark dungeon. Fidelio is a story of liberation. We listened to my father's recording of the opera on many Sunday afternoons for years. The voice of Birgit Nilsson rings in my memory to this day. "Song of the Soul" is a perfect description of the musical experience.

Songs of the soul resound from every religion and ethnological group of humans on earth. The songs are archetypal. The greatest biblical expression of such songs is recorded as The Psalms. Of these, the General Editor of the Jerusalem Bible, Alexander Jones, writes: "…the cries of praise, entreaty and thanksgiving, wrung from the psalmists by events of their own times and by their personal experiences, have a universal note, expressing as they do the attitude that every man should have toward God."[1] Those of us who like myself grew up with the King James Version of the Bible as a transitional object clutched to memory's breast will easily recall, especially in times of mortal stress, the comforting words of the psalmist: "Yea, though I walk through the valley of the shadow of death, I will fear no evil: for thou art with me: thy rod and thy staff, they comfort me. Thou preparest a table before me in the presence of my enemies: thou annointest my head with oil: my cup runneth over. Surely goodness and mercy shall follow me all the days of my life: and I will dwell in the house of the Lord forever."[2] Truly, this is a song of the soul. David, the Old

Testament's Orpheus, could sing the scary beasts of the soul to sleep and transport the listener to a place of peace. Song liberates the soul for life.

In this book, Lena Måndotter offers readers a richly rewarding reflection on the archetypal nature of song. Her words are based securely on her experience as a singer, a songwriter, Jungian psychoanalyst, and a song-therapist. She knows whereof she speaks—from the depths of her being. This work is the harvest of fruit from years of service in the precincts of Orpheus. As I read the text, I can hear her uplifting voice sound across the fields and valleys of her beloved Greece. She is bringing into the world of song her psychological knowledge of the soul, which is also inscribed in the works of her great teacher, C.G. Jung.

Jung, too, was a singer, as witnessed in his now famous Red Book. His Incantations there, performed during a dark night of his soul, yielded the birth of Phanes, a new and also ancient god image, who unites the temporal world of our everyday lives with the eternal world of the soul. Lena's book contributes to our appreciation of this remarkable achievement and is a further gift for our times. She chants the soul alive like the great poets before her.

It is difficult to classify this book. It is inspirational, and it is scholarly; it is a product of Eros and of Logos; it is Apollonic and Dionysian. This combination of qualities slows the reader down to a pace that resembles listening to a song that is being well performed in concert. One must stay with the rhythms and attune the mind to the harmonies, even as one catches the words and meanings. Reading becomes an experience of meditation, of listening for the psyche's response to the words on the page. My recommendation is to take these pages in slowly, and not too many at one sitting. Deep reading is called for here. Not because the ideas are especially complex or difficult, but because a resonance between word and feeling deserves reverberation. It's more like reading poetry than prose. The latter can be skimmed, the former must be slowly savored.

This book is a further volume in the Zurich Lecture Series, which was established at the International School of Analytical Psychology (ISAP) in Zurich, Switzerland, in 2009. The published volumes form the basis for the annual lectures at ISAP during the fall semester. With Lena, this took place in October 2024, and it was exceptional as "lecture" because it combined song and spoken words. This was because the book is a song, and Lena's songs have become a book. Lena is a graduate of the analyst training program at ISAP and thus combines theoretical, clinical and musical gifts in her well-integrated busy life. It was a pleasure to host her and to hear her.

Murray Stein, Ph.D.
Goldiwil, Switzerland

ENDNOTES

[1] The Jerusalem Bible, p. 785.
[2] Psalm 23: 4-6. KJV.

CONTENTS

THE SONG OF THE SOUL
Prelude

"The power of the heart is a secret force or energy which perceives divine realities by a pure hierophanic knowledge without mixture of any kind, because the heart contains even the Divine. In its unveiled state, the heart of the gnostic is like a mirror in which the microcosmic form of the Divine Being is reflected."[1]

HENRY CORBIN

The word 'therapy', in Greek: *therapeuein*, means to 'serve' and 'attend' and the anagram to therapy is *prayeth*. My vocation has been to serve and attend to the sacred – to the world of the soul and its many songs. Using a musical term by the Spanish poet Federico Garcia Lorca[2], I have done what was within my power to serve the *duende*, to attend to the soul's movement by the deep spirit in music. With the French philosopher and theologian Henry Corbin's words, I have entered the *imaginal realm* through song and there my singing soul felt deeply at home.[3]

I have worked as a singer, artist, and song therapist for almost my whole life. Initially I studied to become a performance artist where my creations combined music, poetry, photography, and images. Later I trained as a voice and movement therapist where I worked with groups and individual sessions.[4] Today I use a combination of VMT-techniques with a Jungian approach, and I call this *Song Therapy*. It is an expressive art therapy which means that song can have a cathartic and healing effect if we become emotionally present in our creative acts. In song therapy we focus on perceiving psychological meaning in the sounding of words and attend to deep emotional nuances in the timbre and tone of our voice. I

1

pay as much attention to *how* a word is spoken or sung as to *what* is sung or spoken. I follow each subtle sound of psyche and movement of the body trying to perceive what goes on in our depths, listening to the unconscious in action. In prolonged deep silences I dig for psychic gold.

The English word 'psychotherapy' derives from the Greek language and means "soul-attending," and the ancient Greek word 'psichí' means 'butterfly.' So, when we attend and serve the soul, in one dimension we also attend to the winged flight of the butterfly. The last thing we want to do with the butterfly is to trap it as it then dies. The same will happen to the soul if we try to capture it. How then to write about the soul song without breaking those fragile divine wings?

My creative and therapeutic work in the world of soul and song initially moved me in many different directions. My soul flew like a butterfly and landed wherever she could find nourishing musical nectar. With time I reached the point where I could no longer move horizontally, I was instead forced to move vertically. This meant a deeper descent and a higher ascent so that I could distill what I believe is the essence of my artistic and song-therapeutic work, and how this can nourish Jungian psychoanalytic work. That musical soul essence is what this book is about. At the same time, music will always remain a mystery beyond words and, as musicologist Victor Zuckerkandl wrote: "To assign a definite meaning to music is as impossible as to deny that it is supremely meaningful."[5]

Music can be a healer, but also a wounder – it all depends on the spirit that is put into it. With this I mean that most music (and other arts), lends itself to the composer and performer, and its effect depends on their intent and level of consciousness. Some music is just sedative and seduces us to remain unconscious. Some music manipulates us into various emotional states which is used and taken advantage of by some composers and film directors. Then there are songs that wake us up and touch the soul where deep transformation can happen. These are the songs that interest me. I call them the songs of the soul – they give me hope and keep me singing.

My singing path has been a long and winding one on which I have met many inspiring people, either in person or via their art or their books. To deepen my knowledge of music, I have also kept an eye on recent findings in science and these discoveries have strengthened my faith in the profound power of music and how it relates to the whole cosmos. It appears it all comes down to vibration and resonance, and at its deepest core to musical patterns. "Inside of all particles is a little tiny string that vibrates, sort of like a string on a violin would vibrate... At the heart of matter is music. At the heart of matter are vibrating filaments, vibrating through their sound, matter and energy, maybe even space and time into existence. So there's a real fundamental way in which musical metaphors really brush right up against cutting edge ideas in physics."[6]

Together with my studies in music and psychology, the research and photographic works of Dr Hans Jenny and Alexander Lauterwasser has been an inspiration. Jenny spent most of his life investigating the effect of sound on matter and called his work *Cymatics*. The Greek word 'kýma' means 'wave.' Both Lauterwasser and Jenny have studied the wave phenomena and vibrations of sound manifesting in matter in recurring geometric patterns, similar to those found in nature. Some sounding tones shape and turn materia into cosmic mandalas. By using specific photographic equipment and projecting sound into various forms of matter, such as sand, powder and water, they have been able to make visible these archetypal sound images. Their creative work with Cymatics, their photographs and images, serve as silent visualizations of the mystery of sound.[7]

Since the soul is drawn towards the metaphysical landscape and realm of the gods, I have allowed myself to follow the soul's path into these numinous dimensions. In the musical imaginal realm, I have often found myself in service of Hermes, the divine messenger of music, to whom I will direct some attention in this book. Hermes is a master of crossing boundaries with subtle finesse – he is a transcendent phenomenon. Hermes comes and goes in wandering wonderous ways. He is like the wind – invisible – and I know him only by what he touches, and deep within by what he moves when I sing.

I have lived many years in a mountain village on the island of Crete, and the Greek mythological musician Orpheus has inspired my singing and song-therapeutic work. There are many versions of the myth of

Orpheus, but officially he is best known for losing Eurydice to the underworld and then being killed by the frenzied maenads. I am not sure about this version of the myth anymore since during my research I have found older versions which do not mention this. Instead, I focus on Orpheus as a musician and shaman who used music as soul medicine. His singing and lyre playing enchanted even the gods, and he was blessed with the divine gift of being able to communicate with animals. During all these years of musical practices I have become increasingly aware of why Orpheus needed this special instinctual divine gift.

Singing is not only about musical theory and vocal practices though this is an important part. Singing is also about becoming present in one's heart and in the soul of the song. This requires deep listening, devoted attention, and profound presence. I have chosen to follow Orpheus' musical guidance and have also learnt a great deal from the animal realm since animals are masters of listening, attention, and presence. They carry an instinctual knowledge of musical essentials, and I am grateful for what they have taught me. In this book I will visit the animal realm to seek healing gifts for the singing soul.

To sum up this prelude: it is when I sing that Hermes, Orpheus, the Angels, the Muses, and the spirit of *duende* draw near to my soul. In song I am with them in the holy intermediary realm. In between the songs I sometimes sense them shapeshifting across the seas and sands of the mystical landscapes of psyche. They sometimes also enter my dreams, though these nightly numinous visits are nothing I can command. It is their will, not mine.

In Greek, the word for 'messenger' is 'angelos' and to these divine angelic messengers I dedicate my life and work with devotion. How could I do otherwise? It was they – the numinous messengers – who taught me that the deep song of the soul is true love in musical motion.

ENDNOTES

[1] Henry Corbin, *Alone with the Alone – Creative Imagination in the Sufism of Ibn 'Arabi*, Bollingen Series/Princeton University Press, 1997, p. 222.

[2] Federico Garcia Lorca, *In Search of Duende*, New Direction Books, 1998.

[3] Henry Corbin, *Spiritual Body and Celestial Earth,* Bollingen Series/Princeton University Press, 1989.

[4] For information about Voice Movement Therapy (VMT), see books by Paul Newham: *Therapeutic Voice Work*, *Using Song and Voice in Therapy*, *The Singing Cure* and *The Healing Voice*, and *Singing the Psyche*, ed. Anne Brownell, Deirdre Brownell, and Gina Holloway Mulder.

[5] Victor Zuckerkandl, *The Sense of Music*, Princeton University Press, 1971 (origin. 1959), p. 5.

[6] Brian Greene, expert in the field of string theory, p. 160. Elena Mannes, *The Power of Music – Pioneering Discoveries in the New Science of Song*, Walker Publishing Company, 2011.

[7] For information about Cymatics see: Hans Jenny, *Cymatics – a Study of Wave phenomena and Vibrations* (Vol. 1 & Vol. 2) and Alexander Lauterwasser, *Water Sound Images – The Creative Music of the Universe* (MACROmedia Publishing, www.cymaticsourse.com)

CHAPTER I
The Transpersonal Dimension of Song and Sound

"Hebrew has one single word for both 'spirit' and 'wind' – the word 'ruach'… At the very beginning of creation, before even the existence of the earth or the sky, God is present as a wind moving across the waters."[1]

Angels and Spirits

The air we breathe is essential for all life, and for a singer the breath is crucial to sounding. There are many connections between breath and spirit, but as a singer I tend towards silence, letting the words just rest at the shore instead of speaking of the spiritual dimension of song. In between silences, occasional words come to me, as though I am given them – gifts by winged beings beyond the visual horizon. In the angelic realm I can hear the whispering sound of rustling feathers, the whirling of wild wings.

Henry Corbin writes about the angelic and transcendent form of art:

"The angel of a work, that is to say, its spiritual form, its transcendent content, its trans-natural substance, which, though it cannot be found in the sensuous elements of the work, provides an intimation of the virtualities which transcend them.
To these virtualities we are in every instance called upon to respond, that is, either to assume or reject them, in short, all the spiritual powers of that work (the invisible aspect of a painting, the inaudible

aspect of a symphony), which are not simply the artist's message, but which have been transferred by him to this work and which he himself received from the Angel. To respond to the Angel of a Work is to render oneself capable of the entire content of its aura of love."[2]

These words by Corbin, about the angel of an artistic work, mirrors a humble awareness that an "aura of love" must be present in a transcendent work of art. *True love*. There is also the fact that some artists become instruments which the archetypal powers play upon. We become the servants of song. When we are being moved by these archetypal energies we do not sing. We are being sung by vibrating unspeakable sounds. We do not paint. We are channels through which colours manifest and move. We do not write. We are being thoroughly and wholly written. We do not dance. We are being initiated and danced by divine forces way beyond our intellectual and rational understanding. In other words: one must sing the song until the song starts singing one's very own body, heart, and soul.[3]

Corbin's words about the angel – the divine messenger – of an artistic work, express the same humbleness that Carl Gustav Jung shows in his encounter with the "spirit of the depths." He writes: "...secretly carry your God... conceal the God that you have taken with you... do not speak and do not show the God, but sit in a solitary place and sing incantations in the ancient manner."[4]

Artists who have experienced, and therefore know, that they are only servants and not masters of the divine energies, approach their art in a humble way. In their art the ego is not in charge and in no way does the ego have the final word. The gods are the conductors, and in their musical presence one must bow down low. As Jungian analyst Paul Brutsche writes: "Creativity is a spiritual force that makes use of creative individuals, developing itself through them and making of them vessels of spiritual insight... (and) seen in this light, the creative force is a transpersonal reality."[5]

As an artist I have not been able to create anything of deep soul value unless I have felt this "transpersonal" power rising within me and leaving a feeling of what professor Rudolf Otto calls "mysterium tremendum," the

"Numen."[6] What makes it so difficult for the intellect to grasp is that "while it is complex, it contains a quite specific element or 'moment', which sets it apart from the 'rational'... and which remains inexpressible, an *ineffabile* – in the sense that it completely eludes apprehension in terms of concepts."[7] This *numen* creates within the individual a profound sense of awe and a feeling of being overpowered by a divine majestic power that leaves no choice but to bow down and surrender to its holy presence. In a sense the *numen* is wild and untamed and cannot be imprisoned within the thick walls of religious dogma or psychoanalytical theory. Yet, "There is no religion in which it does not live as the real innermost core, and without it no religion would be worthy of its name."[8]

This experience of a numinous presence cannot be taught, and this resonates with how I feel about the song of the soul. There are some excellent singers who have mastered all the worlds of musical theories and techniques, but who are still not vessels of transpersonal powers. A music colleague of mine described it as: "Listening to them is like looking at a house where all the lights are on, but nobody is at home." Lorca describes such experiences as this: "I used to grow so bored as to feel myself covered in a film of ash about to turn into sneezing powder."[9]

Maybe this is partly about a home-coming, i.e. to come home to one's soul if one is to become an instrument for transpersonal creative forces. Becoming fully present is a non-negotiable request by the Divine; to have a humble attitude and a willingness to make oneself available to something both deeper and higher than the ego will ever know, is a prerequisite. Otto also writes that "strictly speaking, it cannot be taught, it can only be evoked, awakened...as everything that comes 'of the spirit' must be awakened."[10]

In connection to this awakening theme, I would like to return to the title of this chapter and revisit Lorca's description of the Andalusian *Cante Jondo* (Deep Song), and his "theory and play of the Duende."[11] Before we descend into this mystical territory, I need to clarify the etymology of some words which are deeply linked with musical transcendence.

Perhaps some of my thoughts about soul and song can also be applied to Jungian psychoanalysis. Jungian analyst Marie-Louise von Franz emphasizes how important it is for the analyst to become an instrument for transpersonal powers if profound healing is to occur in the analysand. She writes that "… it is essential that the analyst himself have a connection with the numinous and have a belief in it that is based on his own experience."[12] C.G. Jung also directs his attention to the 'numinous' and expresses that "… the main interest of my work is not concerned with the treatment of neuroses, but rather with the approach to the numinous. But the fact is that the approach to the numinous is the real therapy and inasmuch as you attain to the numinous experiences, you are released from the curse of pathology. Even the very disease takes on a numinous character."[13]

To descend vertically into the mystical origins of words I have had to dig down to their etymological roots. It is easy to get lost in the depths of all these roots and their connections. Therefore, I have used some inspiring guidance from philosopher and ecologist David Abram.[14]

The ancient Greek word 'psyche' signifies not only 'soul' or 'butterfly' or 'mind' but also 'breath' and a 'gust of wind.' The word 'psyche' stems from the Greek verb 'psychein' which means 'to breathe' and 'to blow.' The Greek word 'pneuma' means 'spirit' and 'agios pneumatos' means 'holy spirit.' At the same time 'pneuma' also means 'air,' 'wind' and 'breath' and a word like 'pneumonia' derives from this word. This leads us to the association that breathing problems could also be connected to spiritual problems, but this is a discussion that goes beyond the scope of this book.

'Spirit' signifies a vital principle in life and is involved in words like 'respiration' and 'inspiration.' We sometimes also hear people say that they were 'moved by the spirits' which is what Lorca refers to with his concept of *duende* (originally meaning 'duen de' casa: master spirit of the house). In Latin the word for 'spirit' is 'spiritus' and signifies also 'breath' and 'wind' and here one can see that in both Greek and Latin the word for the ethereal spirit is also strongly connected to the body, its breath and the element 'wind.' As pointed out by Abram, God was present as *ruach*, Wind, in the origins of creation.

Jungian analyst and wife of C.G. Jung, Emma Jung, associated music with spirit and wrote in her book *Animus and Anima*:

"… music can be understood as an objectification of the spirit; it does not express knowledge in the usual logical, intellectual sense; it gives sensuous representation to our deepest associations and immutable laws. In this sense, music is spirit, spirit leading into obscure distances beyond the reach of consciousness. Its content can hardly be grasped with words – but strange to say, more easily with numbers – although simultaneously and before else, with feeling and sensation. Apparently paradoxical facts like this show us that music admits us to the depths where spirit and nature are still one – or have again become one. For this reason, music constitutes one of the primordial forms in which woman ever experiences spirit … (and) it may mean a genuine religious experience and then, of course, it is of the highest value."[15]

Abram informs that the Latin word for 'soul' is 'anima' which is at the root of words like 'animal,' 'animation' and 'animism.' The word 'anima' also signifies 'air' and 'breath.' To breathe even more spirit and air into these soul words, the Latin word 'animus' actually derives from the old Greek word for wind: 'anemos.' It might therefore be a good idea to keep in mind that when we deal with soul and spirit, anima and animus, we are having an archetypal encounter with the elemental and natural force of 'Wind.'

Being deeply involved in indigenous oral traditions Abram also tells us that the word 'atmosphere' has its ancestral root in the Sanskrit word 'atman,' "which signified 'soul' as well as 'air' and 'breath'…Words that now seem-to be strictly designated to immaterial mind, or spirit, are derived from terms that once named the breath as the very substance of that mystery…The air was once a singularly sacred presence."

Referring to shamanic song traditions, he writes:

"…the air, we might say, is the soul of the invisible landscape, the secret realm from whence all beings draw their nourishment… the recognition of the air, the wind and the breath as aspects of a singularly sacred power…the Holy wind itself…
And because the Air or Wind is the very medium in which the other natural forces live and act, by transforming the Air through song,

the singer (shaman) is able to affect and subtly influence the activity of the great natural powers themselves…the transforming power of song and prayer."[16]

By entering song as a musical servant, one is given the chance to enter the mystery. That is, if the singer is emotionally and soulfully present, the song will have depth and contain archetypal power. Here we touch upon the unfathomable – the ineffable – where words need musical numinous wings to reach the sublime soul-song essence in flight.

As Henry Corbin writes:
"The mystic must sing in order to say,
since mystical meaning is essentially musical."[17]

Jung also seemed to share Corbin's thoughts about how music is so essential for transmitting the deepest mystical meaning. In a letter to Corbin, he revealed that the words to *Answer to Job* came to him during a high fever and all was accompanied by great music, the music of Bach and Handel. Corbin wrote that he read Jung's book as a musical "oratorio" and Jung replied that while writing he "had the feeling of listening to a great composition, or rather of being at a concert." After Jung had read Corbin's essay "Eternal Sophia," which is a musical intuitive response to *Answer to Job*, he expressed how delighted he was and how it "was an extraordinary joy to me, and not only the rarest of experiences but even a unique experience, to be fully understood… I have received hundreds of critical reviews, but not a single one that comes anywhere near yours in its lucid and penetrating understanding. Your intuition is astounding."[18]

As a musician I read this correspondence between Jung and Corbin as a musical tuning and profound resonance between two souls. They seem to have found each other in the dimension of mystery, their souls felt mirrored and deeply "understood." That is why some musicians always search for the most subtle spiritual tunings, not only of our instruments, but also of our souls. To be deeply and spiritually in tune with someone is – to enter the musical Mysterion.

Holy Spirit and Duende

Living in both Greece and Spain for many years nourished my musical psyche in various ways. Both Mediterranean countries have uniquely captivating and deeply rooted song traditions. In addition, these countries are closely connected to the Oriental music culture which echoes in their songs; the rhythmic subtleties and melodic meanderings that we can hear in Arabic songs.

In Greece I was deeply moved by both the Greek Orthodox prayer tradition and by singers such as Giorgos Dalaras. In his musical pathos and soul presence I sometimes sense Orpheus himself being resurrected. I believe Dalaras has all the artistic duende skills that Lorca spoke about in his book *In Search of Duende*.

I often listened to the old orthodox prayer-songs and tried to learn and recite these holy chants. The Greek orthodox tradition does not dwell more than what is necessary on the crucifixion of the Saviour. Instead, it devotedly prepares for the grand feast celebrating His resurrection. And when the sun rises, the devoted rise in resonance and greet the risen one, and the whole landscape vibrates while they sing *Christos Anesti!*[19]

In Greece, I lived in a small mountain village on the island of Crete. In Spain I also experienced village life and there I witnessed the musical *duende* resounding in rustic cellar-bars in Sevilla and Madrid. All is quite calm and quiet when you get there, but then as night darkens the green earth and the gypsy musicians arrive something out of the ordinary happens. The singing takes on an earthy heart quality that is accompanied by the intense strumming of guitar strings. The musical *cante jondo* séance meanders on hypnotically until suddenly there is an opening into the unspeakable *numen* and tangible *duende* presence. A spontaneous and excited cheer rises from the audience and the syncopated handclapping of the musicians intensifies. Then there is a moment of silence and awe, and within the listener, a sense that the sublime power of the Beyond has entered the 'space' of this ancient cellar.

As a singer I would rather sing and not speak about these numinous moments. My words seem so futile when it comes to what Lorca calls *deep song* and *duende*. So, what did Lorca say? He said that *duende* has to do with dark sounds from the depths of Spirit, a fact he thought is largely ignored by the collective. According to Lorca however, this is the very "substance of art." Quoting Goethe, he wrote that it is a "mysterious force which everyone senses and no philosopher has explained."

In sum, Lorca wrote that it is the "spirit of the earth." A singer must therefore know that the *duende* does not reside in the throat: "...the duende climbs up, inside you, from the soles of the feet." It is truly alive, and it is in the veins of the singer. "It is not a question of ability but of true living style, of blood, of the most ancient culture of spontaneous creation." And "...one must awaken the duende in the remotest mansions of the blood."

The element of 'wind' is present in words like 'psyche,' 'spirit' and 'anima/animus.' Likewise, the word 'duende' resonates with 'wind' and signifies a spirit. Lorca writes:

> "...all of the poems of 'deep song' are magnificently pantheistic;
> the poet asks advice from the wind... entrusts nature with his most
> intimate treasure, completely confident of being listened to.
> One feature of deep song, one admirable poetic reality, is the
> strange way the wind materializes in many of the songs. The wind
> is a character who emerges in the ultimate, most intensely
> emotional moment."[20]

Lorca seems to have mistrusted angels and muses – perhaps he found them too ethereal and unreachable. Instead, he wholeheartedly embraced the earth *duende* daimon and wrote that in seeking the duende, "... there are neither maps nor exercises. We only know he burns the blood like a poultice of powdered glass, that he exhausts, that he rejects all the sweet geometry we have learned."[21]

There are resemblances between Otto and Lorca when they speak about *numen* and *duende*. I believe that the resonance between Otto and Lorca is that they both believed that we cannot transmit duende or numinous powers if we have never experienced these transpersonal forces. Just as Otto writes that one cannot teach *numen* experience, Lorca goes into a holy rage when he writes about musicians who pretend they have *duende*. He writes: "The great artists of the South Spain, whether Gypsy or flamenco, whether they sing, dance, or play, know that no emotion is possible unless the *duende* comes. They may be able to fool people into thinking they have duende—authors, painters, and literary fashion-mongers do so every day—but we have only to pay a little attention, and not surrender to indifference in order to discover the fraud and, chase away their clumsy artifice."[22]

Lorca was a deeply spiritual and subversive poet. No wonder the power ridden fascists shot him at the outbreak of the Spanish civil war. However, in a mercurial way his creations undermined the power of general Franco's soldiers by subversively re-locating the divine soul power in poems way beyond their violent reach. Even if they shot Lorca, the grand poet of Granada, his poems have passed on to the eternal dimension of immortality. You can shoot the poet, but you cannot shoot the poem.[23]

The Canadian poet and singer Leonard Cohen was as a young Jewish man profoundly moved when he first encountered Lorca's poems. The spirit of the poems touched Cohen's soul just as deeply as the power and beauty of the Hebrew prayers recited in the synagogue had done. The poetic universe of Lorca seemed very familiar to him, and by reading the poems and absorbing the *numen* of the words he was no longer alone. He was held by the *duende* illuminating his inner landscape and interior horizon.[24]

When Leonard Cohen was awarded the Prince of Asturias Award 2012, he said: "Poetry comes from a place that no one commands, and no one conquers." And, he expressed his deep gratitude to Lorca with the following words:

"It was only when I read, even in translation, the works of Lorca that I understood that there was a voice. It is not that I copied his voice; I would not dare. But he gave me permission to find a voice, to locate a voice, that is to locate a self, a self that is not fixed, a self that struggles for its own existence."

15

The Prayer of the Heart

"The cultural technique of deep attention emerged precisely out of ritual and religious practices… Every religious practice is an exercise in attention…(and) attention is the natural prayer of the soul… The expression 'to learn something by heart,' like the French 'apprendre par Coeur,' tells us that apparently only repetition reaches the heart… Repetition stabilizes and deepens attention… Repetition differs from routine in its capacity to create intensity."[25]

Prayer-song is a precise mode of singing – a coherent musical mode of being. To enter the singing mode of prayer requires devotion and deep listening, acute attention, and profound heart-presence. For the prayer to have a transcendent resonance within our being, within our soul it needs to be repeated, and this musical repetition takes as much place in the heart as it does in the brain. We do not say that we learn the words, or the song, 'by brain,' we say we learn it 'by heart.' This is a crucial aspect to be aware of if we want to experience the transpersonal dimension of song.

Each round of repetition brings the singer deeper and deeper into the world of vibration and resonance. For this to have a healing effect, the singer must feel and express these feelings. That is when the prayer-song can have a cathartic function and become a way to experience the *numen*. If the singer is just sounding without deep heart presence, the song is just a song.

Science has been focused on discovering what happens in the brain when we sing and listen to music. Some of those scientific findings are very interesting and show how we can benefit from music and singing, both physically and psychologically. But what about the heart? Fortunately, there has been some scientific research done on the heart which shows that the heart is a mysterious and enigmatic organ that has its own way of perceiving and remembering. Some of the most important scientific discoveries show that the heart can direct the brain and that the heart carries memories. Most astounding are the memories that surface in people who have had heart transplants. Once the new heart is in place, some people start remembering the heart donor's life, both the good and the bad.[26]

The deepest and most transformative way for my heart to enter the land of the sacred is through song. As Llewellyn Vaughan-Lee writes "The repetition of sacred words strengthens our remembrance of God and helps to awaken the Divine within our heart…this awakening within the heart, this birth of continual prayer, is one of the miracles of the path…the heart is a place of prayer, an altar of love."[27] The older I have become it is in the imaginal land of prayers that my soul has found its true home. I use the word "imaginal" in the same sense as Corbin, i.e., the imaginal is a *real* world, it is neither an imaginary world nor a fantasy. Our heart is the subtle organ that perceives this reality of the soul, it is not our intellect, and it is not our senses.

Being moved and enchanted by the prayers of the world does not prevent me from excursions into other musical genres and soundscapes. I am moved if I feel the subtle vibration which serves both the depths and the heights of the spirit. With prayer I do not necessarily mean only traditional uplifting songs since in the world of art we must also allow for periods of destruction for the sake of transformation and re-creation. Quoting the Bible, singing is what can bring down the walls. Sometimes the Blues can have a cathartic effect, and at other times a dark rock song will bring back the light. When we are sad and listen to a singer who is as sad as we are, we are no longer alone, we are no longer an isolated person. We are in communion with and in the company of another human being – mirrored and soulfully witnessed.

There are also transformational energies in songs of lament. When we can feel and express our deepest despair, and authentically sing our unspeakable sorrow, we enable the healing of our soul and the emergence of the new. The song of lament becomes the bridge over the abyss of sorrow, the bridge which we are invited to cross.

With prayer I mean a profound musical calling from the depth of the soul, be it an Andalusian "cante jondo," a wild hard rock ballad or a dark gospel to the lord. Prayer for me is not only about 'what,' it is also about 'how' and 'from where' does this voice and song emerge. Not always, but at certain moments of grace, the monks of Einsiedeln when chanting "Salve Regina" to the holy Black Madonna also reconnect to that musical spirit. With Lorca's words, when the *duende* comes we are being soulfully stirred and feel as though we are "baptized by dark waters."[28]

Our voices and our songs are transcendent instruments for entering the world of the sacred. Since time immemorial shamans have known the curative power of chants and "both music and song have been used as a healing agent by different cultures across the world since the earliest times" and these shamanic traditions show "the crucial role of the human voice in the process of healing."[29]

The internationally renowned song teacher Alfred Wolfsohn, who was greatly interested in the works of Jung, directed strong attention to this numinous power of song. At the end of his book, Wolfsohn expresses how moved he was by singing prayers. He was not the one to ignore the shadow of the voice and all the emotional pain that the wounded psyche needs to express in sounds and songs. He even healed himself from traumatic war memories by loudly re-sounding his torturing aural memories of the screams of dying soldiers in the trenches. However, in the final analysis, it seems as though all journeys in his song-therapeutic life, led Wolfsohn to one single voice, the voice of God.

> *"Roused by the power of song which is the breath of God,*
> *I saw and heard the flowers, the trees, stones, water, mountains,*
> *the very earth, move and sing.*
> *Then all of a sudden, I beheld the vault of Heaven as one huge*
> *resonant body.*
> *I saw the clouds as bows playing this immense celestial violin,*
> *bringing forth new melodies*
> *and in the space between the heavens above and the earth below,*
> *I heard but one voice;*
> *the voice of God."*[30]

So why is the singing soul so deeply drawn to the prayer of the divine dawn? Corbin seems to have had a precise musical ear and this can also be noted in the inherent musicality in his writings. Sometimes it seems as though he wrote from within the imaginal and musical sphere. His sentences have a profound melodic prosody, and it is not only the tonality and rhythms of the sentences – it is his invisible musical presence within the words.

I feel that the words by Corbin here below are subversive instruments in the battle for the song of the soul of the world.

> *"For prayer is not a request for something: it is the expression of a mode of being… Prayer is the highest form, the supreme act of the Creative Imagination… visible to the heart, to the Active Imagination…is the worshiper's being in the measure of its capacity. God prays for us…which means that He epiphanizes himself insofar as He is the God 'whom' and 'for whom' we pray... We do not pray to the Divine Essence in its hiddenness; each faithful ('abd) prays to 'his' Lord ('Rabb'), the Lord who is in the form of his faith."*[31]

ENDNOTES

[1] David Abram, *The Spell of the Sensuous – Perception and Language in a More-Than-Human World*, Vintage Books/Random House, 1997, p. 239.

[2] Henry Corbin, *Alone with the Alone – Creative Imagination in the Sufism of Ibn 'Arabi*, Bollingen Series/Princeton University Press, 1997, p. 291.

[3] See also the film: *Letters to a Young Singer* by Lena Måndotter, Kameleont Production 2009.

[4] Carl Gustav Jung, *The Red Book* (Liber Novus), ed. Sonu Shamdasani, *The Foundation of the Works of C.G. Jung*, W.W. Norton & Company, 2009. (Philemon Foundation), p. 298.

[5] Paul Brutsche, *Creativity – Patterns of Creative Imagination as Seen Through Art*, Spring Journal Books, 2018, p. 252.

[6] Rudolf Otto, *The Idea of the Holy, an Inquiry into the Non-rational Factor in the Idea of the Divine and its relation to the Rational*, Penguin Books, 1959. p. 26.

[7] Ibid., p. 19.

[8] Ibid., p. 20.

[9] Federico Garcia Lorca, *In Search of Duende*, New Directions Publ., 1998, p. 56.

[10] Rudolf Otto, *The Idea of the Holy*, p. 21.

[11] Federico Garcia Lorca, *In Search of Duende*, p. 1 and p. 56.

[12] Marie Louise von Franz, *Psychotherapy*, Shambhala Publications, 1993, p. 179.

[13] Carl Gustav Jung, *Selected Letters 1909 - 1961*, Princeton University Press, 1984, p. 62.

[14] David Abram, *The Spell of the Sensuous - Perception and Language in a More-than-Human World*, Vintage Books/Random House, 1997.

[15] Emma Jung, *Animus and Anima*, Spring Publications, 2008, pp. 36 - 37.

[16] David Abram, *The Spell of the Sensuous*, pp. 226 - 240.

[17] Henry Corbin, *The Voyage and the Messenger*, North Atlantic Books, 1998, p. 235.

[18] Carl Gustav Jung, *Letters Volume 2: 1951 – 1961*, ed. Gerhard Adler/Aniela Jaffé, transl. R F C Hull, Routledge, 1990.

[19] See also music album, Lena Måndotter, the Greek prayer-song "Christos Anesti".

[20] Federico Garcia Lorca, *In Search of Duende*, pp. 17 - 18.

[21] Ibid., pp. 56 – 72.

[22] Ibid., p. 60.

[23] See music album *Prayers and Prophecies – Live at the Palladium*, (a recital of Lorca's poem La Guitarra. Lena Måndotter - vocals, Pierre Engström - guitar).

[24] Sylvie Simmons, *I'm Your Man – The Life of Leonard Cohen*, Vintage Books/Random house, 2013, p. 29.
For Leonard Cohen's speech at the award ceremony: https://www.youtube.com/watch?v=Pnx20BZquAo

[25] Byung-Chul Han, *The Disappearance of Rituals – a Topology of the Present*, Polity Press, 2020, p. 8.

[26] For more information on the science of the heart see website HeartMath Institute and the books by Paula M Reeves, *Heart Sense*, Stephen Harrod Buhner, *The Secret Teachings of Plants – The Intelligence of the Heart* and *Plant Intelligence and the Imaginal Realm* and Anne Elizabeth Taylor, *Unveiling Sophia – Heart Wisdom in an Age of Technology*.

[27] Llewellyn Vaughan-Lee, *Prayer of the Heart in Christian & Sufi Mysticism*, The Golden Sufi Center, 2017, p. XXV, p. 80 – 81 and Henry Corbin's prelude to, *Spiritual Body and Celestial Earth*.

[28] Federico Garcia Lorca, *In Search of Duende*, p. 67.

[29] Paul Newham, *The Singing Cure*, Shambhala Publications. 1993, p. 46.

[30] Alfred Wolfsohn, *Orpheus – or the Way to a Mask*, Abraxas Publishing, 2012, p. 158.

[31] Henry Corbin, *Alone with the Alone*, p. 248. See also Lena Måndotter's music albums for prayer-songs.

CHAPTER II
Sound and Psyche

Performance and Ritual

"What these mystics have produced is the equivalent to what is called sacred music.
The reason for this is so profound, that to understand it is to see that all music can only appear as sacred, provided that it surrenders itself to its supreme finality."[1]

The divine creative imagination within, and the soul-dimension of life, is seriously threatened in our modern rational world of mechanistic, statistical thinking and the collective idolatry of so called 'reason.'[2] Corbin wrote that we must counteract this collective "agnostic reflex." Through my artistic and therapeutic work, I try to defend the wounded world of the soul. Many clients who come to me have suffered from a serious lack of meaning in life, and a severely broken connection to their souls and to the world of the spirit of the depths. In my practice I have found that under many psychological and physiological symptoms there can be deeper traumatic spiritual problems of the soul. The soul has its own way of defending itself, but it can also go into deep hiding. Orpheus knew how to do shamanic soul retrievals and he knew the magic of music. The soul is enchanted by music and luminous colors, and through singing and painting we can bring soul back.[3]

Therapeutically touching upon the soul's wound often brings up dark grief, but the cleansing tears allow for new psychic energy to enter back into our lives. Sometimes we suffer not only our own personal wounds, but also, without us being aware of it, we carry the weight of collective psychic wounds. If the ego has a weak sense of boundaries, the unexpressed shadow of the collective can enter us. This happens not only to artists, but it can also happen to anyone. To give creative visual and audible form to what the unconscious brings up in us, can help us in our healing process – we can then see and feel in our paintings and our songs what is moving within us. We learn to discern which wound is mine and which wound is thine. This approach resonates with Jung who emphasized that he always tried to serve the analysand in a way that "archetypal" healing could take place since he thought that a cure on an archetypal level was deeper and more permanent.

To attend to the sacred also means to serve the gods. This places the singer and song therapist in a position of service, at a deeper level than the human ego might be willing to go. When I was younger, I worked as an artist, musician, photographer, and poet in the world of experimental and ritual performance. Later, I took a long break from the performance world and solely focused on giving concerts.[4] The years of work with performances offered a free space to explore the intermediary realm between art and therapy, and performance and ritual, in which the audiences sometimes joined in as participants. Looking back, I can see that the numinous power of sound was always at the centre of my creative work even though there was also a strong focus on image and word. I learned a lot about therapy through art, and I learned a lot about art through therapy.

Throughout my life I have longed for a deep connection to my soul so that I can serve the Anima Mundi – the Soul of the World. I allowed my curiosity to take me on many artistic adventures and found teachers or teachings that deepened my own creative work. Some of these teachers I met, or I trained with their disciples. Sometimes numinous books came my way and moved me into new creative dimensions.[5]

The musical longing of my soul required of me to also study song and music, theoretically and practically, and to learn the art of presence, attention, and other artistic skills. There was always a mystery involved in learning songs since I experienced them as animated beings coming my way. I often felt that the songs chose me instead of me choosing them. It was a calling, and a feeling that something would be revealed if I learned the song. I never thought of songs as just rhythms and melodies. I always felt that I would enter something more profound, and that 'it' would also enter me, the more acquainted I became with the song.

Polish theatre director Jerzy Grotowski had a keen interest in song and singing and worked with theatre "as vehicle." He focused on the vertical ladder, the vertical psychic process within the actor, an evocation of the profound dimensions of sounding a song. Since learning ritual songs of ancient traditions has always moved my soul, I would like to share some of what Grotowski writes:

> *"The ritual songs of the ancient tradition give support in the construction of the rungs of the vertical ladder. It is not a question only of capturing the melody with its precision, even if without this nothing is possible. It is also necessary to find a tempo-rhythm with all its fluctuations inside the melody. But above all, it is a question of something that constitutes the proper sonority: vibratory qualities which are so tangible that in a certain way they become the meaning of the song.*
>
> *In other words, the song becomes the meaning in itself through the vibratory qualities; even if one doesn't understand the words, reception alone is enough. When I speak of this 'meaning,' I speak at the same time of the impulses of the body; that is, the sonority and the impulses are the meaning, directly.*
>
> *To discover the vibratory qualities of a ritual song of an ancient tradition, it is necessary to discover the difference between the melody and the vibratory qualities. This is very important in societies in which the oral transmission has disappeared. For this reason, it is important to us. In our world, in our culture one understands, for example, the melody as a succession of notes, a notation of notes. This is the melody.*

> *It is not possible to discover the vibratory qualities of the song if one begins, let's say, to improvise; I don't mean that one sings out of tune, but, if one sings the same song five times and each time a different one appears, it means that the melody has not been fixed. The melody should be totally dominated, in order that one can develop the work on vibratory qualities."*[6]

When we deal with song and music on an archetypal level, we are encountering vibratory qualities and subtle shifts in tonal and harmonic resonances. This is an encounter with the enigma of psychic energy and numinous presence. Pure presence can be experienced as a deep musical reverberation and a channeling of increased intensity of libido – life energy. We are trying to sound the mana of the Mysterion. One must empty oneself of what stands in the way of this – it is a *via negativa*. Theatre director Peter Brook writes: "To understand this in terms of an art, we will need to see very precisely what elements create this movement of life – and which one prevent it from appearing. The fundamental element is the body."[7] The soul dwells within the body and we can therefore assume that to reveal the "holy invisible" requires the presence and attention of soul, and an instinctual awareness in our body.

Singing is as much about listening as it is about the sounding musical act of performing. Listening with soul is a profound art and being receptive to sound has both psychological and musical aspects. "A person can only produce vocally what he is capable of hearing" writes Dr Alfred Tomatis, who has helped many singers to focus on the "conscious ear."[8]

Jungian analyst Mary Lynn Kittelson suggests that we should try to become more advanced auditory beings, not only visually orientated. She writes that "in seeking for the depths, vision is not necessarily the sensory channel of choice. In the deep, in the underworld, in dreams, the search is for resonance. It is for meaning beyond appearance." And since the ear is a labyrinth "the auditory perception resists the direct pathway. Its ways are labyrinthine, echoic. Its essence is vibration, resonance."[9]

With the song of the soul, we must try to develop a deeper, sublime sense of listening, a "listening to the secret movements of the hidden process."[10]

The Sufi musician Hazrat Inayat Khan writes that "other sounds can be louder than the voice, but no sound can be more living."[11] He also means that the "true use of music is to become musical in one's thoughts, words and action… and it is the state of vibrations to which man is tuned that accounts for his soul's note… and some day in the future music will be the means of expressing universal religion."

After having listened to primordial voice and song of the Australian aboriginals, Bruce Chatwin wrote about their song lines and ancient dreaming tracks. "Aboriginal Creation myths tell of the legendary totemic beings who have wandered over the continent in Dreamtime, singing out the name of everything that crossed their path – birds, animals, plants, rocks, waterholes – and so singing the world into existence."[12]

In a similar spirit Abram writes about the power of the instinctual voice, the ancient oral traditions in connection to archetypal memory and the language of the land, and the memory and dreamtime stories and songs:

> "The Dreaming songs provide an auditory mnemonic (or memory tool) – an oral means of recalling viable routes through an often harsh terrain…The chanting of particular songs is itself prompted by the sensible encounter with specific sites. Just as the song structure carries the memory of how to orient in the land, so the sight of particular features of the land activates the memory of specific songs and stories. The landscape itself, then, provides a visual mnemonic, a set of visual cues for remembering the Dreamtime stories."[13]

The songs and the sounds of the soul have always been of spiritual value to humanity, and music is at the core of many religious traditions. Originally, songs were considered healing agents and were therefore treated as sacred. Singing moved us into the world of the gods where deep transformation could take place. When the archetypal powers entered the words, they were transformed and became prayers, and when the praying words could no longer contain the powerful numinous energies, the prayer shifted and metamorphosed into song. At this stage the song became a transcendent sounding container, an alchemical musical vessel for divine vibrations.

Across the ages, mystics within most religions have always used sound and song to enter communion and resonance with the Divine. There comes a time however when even the most spiritual songs will turn back towards home, to their musical birthplace in the archetypal realm and be seized by the eternal silence. Until that moment comes, one can do nothing but sing. That moment in time comes of its own accord. Until then, the soul will keep on sounding the Mysterion.

Philosopher Gershom Scholem writes:

"Mystical experience is fundamentally amorphous. The more intensely and profoundly the contact with God is experienced, the less susceptible it is of objective definition, for by its very nature it transcends the categories of subject and object which every definition presupposes... Because mystical experience as such is formless, there is in principle no limit to the forms it can assume. At the beginning of their path, mystics tend to describe their experience in forms drawn from the world of perception. At later stages, corresponding to different levels of consciousness, the world of nature recedes, and these 'natural' forms are gradually replaced by specifically mystical structures. Nearly all mystics describe such structures as configurations of lights and sounds. At still later stages, as the mystic's experience progresses towards the ultimate formlessness, these structures dissolve in their turn... For light and sound and even the name of God are merely symbolic representations of an ultimate reality which is unformed, amorphous."[14]

Jung and Music

"The sea is like music.
It has all the dreams of the soul within itself and sounds them over."[15]

Jung seemed to care deeply for music. Perhaps he cared so much that he could not listen to music for very long as he thought that "music is dealing with such deep archetypal material, and many of those who play don't realize this." Even though Jung was more visually oriented himself, and used painting rather than music in his active imaginations, he wrote:

"Music expresses in sounds what fantasies and visions express in visual images… I can only draw your attention to the fact that music represents the movement, development, and trans-formations of the motifs of the collective unconscious.[16]

After having met the music therapist Margaret Tilly in 1956, Jung also pointed at the therapeutic value of song and music:

"I feel that from now on music should be an essential part of every analysis. Music reaches the deep archetypal material that we can only sometimes reach in our analytical work with patients. This is most remarkable."[17]

What could it mean in the space of Jungian analysis, or for that matter any therapy, when Jung proposes that "music should be an essential part of every analysis?" I do not have the definitive answer to this, but I do believe it could be useful to initially integrate more music and song in the therapeutic training programs. By doing this the future of therapy and psychoanalysis could make use of song and music as healing tools which can benefit the souls and bodies of the clients. In the same way we use dream symbols, art and painting in our active imaginations, we can use song and music.

I recall reading that Jung, in one of his sessions, sang to his client and how his singing cured her from her emotional distress. Jung discovered the cure his singing had brought about when he met the doctor who had referred the client to him. The doctor had been very surprised and wanted to know more about what Jung had done to transform the psyche of this client. This is a story about how song can be a therapeutic container for numinous healing energies, and this is what Jung told the doctor:

"How was I to explain to him that I had simply listened to something within myself?... I began, almost without doing it on purpose, to hum what I was telling her about the wind, the waves, the sailing, and relaxation, to the tune of the little lullaby. I hummed those sensations, and I could see that she was 'enchanted'...

"I was quite at sea. How was I to tell him that I had sung her a lullaby with my mother's voice? Enchantment like that is the oldest form of medicine. But it all happened outside of my reason: it was not until later that I thought about it rationally and tried to arrive at the laws behind it. She was cured by the grace of God."[18]

Sounding and Wording

"Many investigators assume that human speech was originally a sort of chant, and that it was only in the course of evolution that the two branches separated into the language of words and the language of tones. The world of man has never been without tone."[19]

One important aspect of sound is that it is a direct expression of the psychic energy of the emotion whereas a word is not. A word is a description of the emotion, a certain combination of letters that we humans have agreed will mean this or that. By this I propose that sounds can reach a deeper part of our psyche than words can do. For people who have lived their whole lives overly dependent on their intellect, entering the world of sound can bring deep relief and peace to the soul. Some psychic wounds are unspeakable, but they are not unsoundable.

In my world of sound, I often find that words can limit the many dimensions of the soul's reality. Unless words create poems, of course, but that is another psychic dimension. Jungian analyst Nancy Krieger describes this limiting process as follows: "An idea starts first as an image before it is translated into language… The process of putting an idea into words fixes one meaning and excludes the others to the unconscious."[20]

Jung illuminates us on the origins of language:

"Language was originally a system of emotive and imitative sounds… sounds which imitate the noises of the elements, the rushing of the gurgling of water, the rolling of thunder, the roaming of the wind, the cries of the animal world… And lastly, those which represent a combination of the sound perceived and the emotional reaction to it... Thus language, in its origin and essence is simply a system of signs and symbols that denote real occurrences or their echo in the human soul… The most abstract system of philosophy is, in its method and purpose, nothing more than an extremely ingenious combination of natural sounds."[21]

I always try to remember these words by Jung when I work with clients as there is a substantial amount of communication going on in the non-verbal space. In this space one can feel the depth of the emotions that might be lost when the clients are struggling to verbalize what they really feel, i.e. parts of their feelings can get lost on their way into words. I often sense a mutual resonance in this wordless dimension, and clients feel musically mirrored in both silence and sound. Sound is a potential vehicle to the imaginal realm and, as Jungian dance and drama therapist Penny Lewis writes, "sound permeates through body boundaries and intellectual defenses, it is often considered the most basic form of connecting and communing in the imaginal realm."[22]

Paul Newham describes humanity's historical development from emotive communication to cognitive communication and the psychic and musical price it has paid in the process. According to Newham it is a development from "the phono-physical voice-dance to verbal linguistics," and what the voice loses along the way is spontaneity, emotional connection and resonance, tonal musical variety, and soulful presence.

> *"With the development of words, this sympathetic relationship with the world gradually disappeared, not least because the sung tones of affect and experience became appropriated by a spoken code of linguistics. The acoustic composition of words became more and more abstracted from the essence of that which they sought to express, so that eventually it was not necessary to experience and embody something in order to make it the subject of com-munication...*
>
> *In the course of this development, it became unnecessary for people to experience the essence of a subject in order to express and so identify it. People did not need to experience and embody the essence of fear or triumph, or a bear or a horse, the river or the night in order to communicate about them, for the words which had come to stand in their place were understood abstractly. Human-kind had ceased to express through sound and begun to describe with words."*[23]

Extensive research among children who have no formal musical training shows that many of these children have a greater capacity for spontaneous musical compositions than children who are formally and theoretically trained. It is as though their musical intellectual cognition stands in the way of the instinctual creative flow. Professor of psychology Howard Gardner points out:

> *"Although the mastery of any symbolic system takes years, I do not feel that a new order of mechanisms comes into play at specifiable times. The groupings, groups and operation described by Piaget do*

not seem essential for mastery or understanding of human language, music, or the plastic arts. Rather the organism's experience with these symbol systems involves an increasingly complex making, perceiving, and feeling, which draws in a comprehensive way on the mechanisms evolved during infancy. The rate at which a child becomes able to manipulate tones, words, or lines varies greatly, but logical operations play little or no role in these activities. Development takes place within the medium itself, through a concrete exploration and amplification of its properties. Just as there is no need to step outside the medium, there is no need for the artist, performer, or audience member to master logical operations, or to pass through the cognitive landmarks that occupy Piaget."[24]

I find it inspiring to read about the different modes of human cognition and communication. It also helps me to embrace the many facets of the psyche in my work with clients. As an artist I often feel an ambivalence regarding words and theories. Philosopher Susanne Langer divided the process of human communication into two modes – discursive and non-discursive. When referring to the limits of discursive mode and the opening to the non-discursive mode, she believed that "in the physical, space-time world of our experience there are things which do not fit the grammatical scheme of expression. But they are not necessarily blind, inconceivable, mystical affairs; they are simply matters which require to be conceived through some symbolistic schema other than discursive language." Langer was interested in how artists perceive and express their art and considered that: "The tonal structures we call 'music' bear a close logical similarity to the forms of human feeling…(to) the greatness and brevity and eternal passing of everything vitally felt. Such is the pattern, or logical form, of sentience; and the pattern of music is that same form worked out in pure, measured sound and silence. Music is a tonal analogue of emotive life."[25]

When I write I can feel not only inspired, but also afraid that I, in essence, might do harm to the subject I am writing about. With this I mean that when my words emerge and manifest there is a risk that in their verbal emergence the words will leave some subtle soul-essence behind in the nonverbal space. An image that comes to my mind is a collection of butterflies. The collector has put them in a neat order, one shiny needle through each little winged being and then framed them tightly behind glass. At first glance it all looks very beautiful but, in truth, the butterflies are all dead.

When writing I also miss the wild animal's or playful child's pure sounding space where the instinctual sounds carry more meaning than human words. During the years 2010-2011, I was supervised in my song therapy work by the late Jungian analyst and musician Mario Jacoby. About the limiting power of language, he wrote:

"Language is a double-edged sword. On the one hand, it enriches the field of common experience; on the other hand, it limits it. Only part of the original, global experience can be expressed in words. The rest remains inaccurately named and poorly understood. Many other realms remain likewise unexpressed, left to lead a nameless, but nonetheless real existence. Language thus drives a wedge between two modes of experience: one that can only be lived directly and another that can be verbally represented. To the extent that experience is connected to words, the growing child becomes shut off from the spontaneous flow of experience that characterized the preverbal state. Thus, a child gains entry into its culture at the cost of losing the robustness and wholeness of its original experience." [26]

ENDNOTES

[1] Henry Corbin, *The Voyage and the Messenger*, p. 231.

[2] John Ralston Saul, *Voltaires Bastards – the Dictatorship of Reason in the West*, Simon & Schuster, 1992. Annie Le Brun, *The Reality Overload – the Modern World's Assault on the Imaginal Realm*, Inner Traditions, 2008. Gary Lachman, *Lost Knowledge of the Imagination*, Floris Books, 2020. Kathleen Raine, all her books.

[3] Donald Kalshed, *Trauma and the Soul*, Routledge, 2013, Eric Neumann, *Art and the Creative Unconscious*, Princeton University Press, 1959, 3rd ed. 1974, (Bollingen Foundation), Albert Kreinheder, *Body and Soul – the Other Side of Illness*, Inner City Books, orig. 1991, 2nd ed. 2009.

[4] Most of the performances and audio-visual installations were shown at Malmö Konsthall, one of Northern Europe's largest spaces for contemporary art. Some of the scenic compositions toured nationally and internationally. See www.lenamandotter.com

[5] My artistic and song therapeutic work was initially inspired by trainings with writer and voice- and movement therapist Paul Newham, Jungian analyst and film-director Ingela Romare and Jungian analyst and writer Marion Woodman, and many singers and songwriters such as Giorgos Dalaras and Leonard Cohen. Though we never met, I found Anna Halprin's dance therapy and theatre director Peter Brook's work very interesting, especially Halprin's belief in dance as a healing agent and Brook's innovative approach to voice and sound. Shaun McNiff's soulful approach to art and healing has also been a great inspiration

[6] Thomas Richards, *At Work with Grotowski*, Routledge, 1995, pp. 126 - 127.

[7] Peter Brook, *There Are No Secrets – Thoughts on Acting and Theatre*, Methuen Drama, 1995, p. 17.

[8] Alfred Tomatis, *The Conscious Ear – My Life of Transformation Through Listening*, Station Hill Press, 1991, p. XII.

[9] Mary Lynn Kittelson, *Sounding the Soul – the Art of Listening*, Daimon, 1996, p. 13.

[10] Peter Brook, *There are No Secrets – Thoughts on Acting and Theatre*, p. 119.

[11] Hazrat Inayat Khan, *The Music of Life,* Omega Publications, 1983, p. 93.

[12] Bruce Chatwin, *The Songlines*, Penguin Books, 1988, p. 2.

[13] David Abram, *The Spell of the Sensuous*, Vintage Books/Random House, 1997, p. 175.

[14] Gershom Scholem, *On the Kabbalah and its Symbols*, (transl. Ralph Manheim), Schocken Books, 1996, p. 8.

[15] Carl Gustav Jung, *Memories, Dreams, Reflections*, p. 369.

[16] Carl Gustav Jung, *Letters Vol. 1*, ed. Gerhard Adler and Aniela Jaffé, Routledge, p. 542.

[17] Carl Gustav Jung, ed. McGuire & Hull, *C.G. Jung Speaking*, p. 275.

[18] Carl Gustav Jung, *C.G. Jung Speaking*, ed. McGuire & Hull, pp. 418 - 419.

[19] Victor Zuckerkandl, *Sound and Symbol – Music and the Eternal World*, Princeton University Press, 1973 (orig. 1956) p. 1.

[20] Nancy Krieger, *Bridges to Consciousness – complexes and complexity*, Routledge, 2014, p. 159.

[21] Carl Gustav Jung, *Symbols of Transformation*, Collected Works Vol. 5, Princeton University Press, 1956, pp. 12 - 13.

[22] Penny Lewis, *Creative Transformation: The Healing Power of the Arts*, Chiron Publications, 1993, p. 25.

[23] Paul Newham, *The Singing Cure*, p. 24.

[24] Howard Gardner, *The Arts and Human Development – A Psychological Study of the Artistic Process*, Basic Books, 1994, p. 45. See also Howard Gardner's Project Zero at Harvard University, which investigates the non-logical process of artistic creativity and development.

[25] Susanne K. Langer, *Philosophy in a New Key – A Study in the Symbolism of Reason, Rite, and Art*, Harvard University Press, 1957, p. 88 and *Feeling and Form – A Theory of Art*, Charles Scribner's Sons, 1953, p. 27.

[26] Mario Jacoby, *Jungian Psychotherapy & Contemporary Infant Research*, Routledge, 1999, p. 53.

CHAPTER III
Hermes – Guide of Soul and Song

"He will make you a witness of the mysteries of God and the secrets of nature."[1]

I have dedicated many of my performances to a series of archetypal beings and having lived many years in the Cretan mountains of Greece, it felt natural to attend to some of the ancient Greek gods and mythological figures. Some of my musical performances were created in the form of a ritual – in a *temenos*[2] which is in line with the shamanic and prophetic traditions of ancient Greece.[3] I was inspired by the Greek shamanic singer *Orpheus*, the Greek goddess of memory, *Mnemosyne*, the goddesses of crossroads and underworlds, *Hecate and Persephone*, and the Trojan seeress and oracle *Cassandra*. As an archetypal background to all my creative and therapeutic work my soul has found strength by staying in tune with *Hermes*, the psychopomp of the underworld and the divine messenger between humans and the gods.[4]

Hermes is the magical musician whom we can experience as a numinous presence in the archetypal background of all our artistic creations and song therapies. He is an enchanting, winged, mysterious messenger and remembering this can bring more vital energy to our lives. As a singer and a performance artist I often enter my preparatory work in circumambulation around the most numinous images that my soul gifts me. This I do to distill the psychic essence that guides my music and the direction of my soul. To demonstrate what I mean: I enter the world of Hermes, an active imagination, where he can speak to and through me, and perhaps reach you, the reader, in your own creative space of hermetic listening.

Before we enter the world of Hermes, I would just like to emphasize – Hermes is *real*. He is not a fantasy. He is a tangible presence in the imaginal realm. When we enter this divine dimension, we need to use the subtle perception of our soul, not our intellect and not our senses. We are journeying beyond reductive concepts. Jung describes the real and profound presence of his soul guide Philemon as follows:

> *"(Philemon) brought home the crucial insight that there are things in the psyche which I do not produce, but which produce themselves and have their own life. Philemon represented a force which was not myself ... I held conversations with him, and he said things which I had not consciously thought. For I observed clearly that it was he who spoke, not I ... It was he (Philemon) who taught me psychic objectivity, the reality of the psyche. Through him the distinction was clarified between myself and the object of my thought. He confronted me in an objective manner, and I understood that there is something in me which can say things that I do not know and do not intend, things which may even be directed against me."*[5]

Our eyes may not be able to see Hermes in the bright light of our day-to-day world, but our souls may perceive this musical mercurial messenger in the twilight space between worlds; in a moonlit landscape where the veils are thin; in the dimension that Corbin calls the *Mundus Imaginalis*. It is "a very precise order of reality, which corresponds to a precise mode of perception."[6]

Hermes lives in the imaginal realm, situated between our sensuous and intellectual perception. If we can connect our artistic and therapeutic work to this imaginal world, things come alive, the soul awakens, and we experience a suprasensory dimension full of ancient, winged wisdom – if only we humbly attend to and serve it with our souls. Professor Antoine

Faivre expands on the theme of *creative imagination*, on Corbin's theme of the *imaginal realm*, and Jung's theme of *imaginatio activa*, and notes:

> *"In theosophies, that imagination is supposed to enable one to have access to the intermediate realm – a mesocosmos between the divine and Nature – that is, to those of the 'subtle bodies,' angelic and archetypal entities… The creative imagination is the visionary faculty that enables one to grasp the multileveled meanings of reality i.e., of the Holy Writ and of the Book of Nature."*[7]

I will embark on the journey of a singer and allow myself a hermetic voyage of "poetic imagination and reverie."[8] But then, how to journey back with Hermes to his musical mysterious source?[9]

The world of music can bring profound and mysterious experiences which are not easily described in words. Hermes is a mercurial guide who by divine grace brings the musical and spiritual mystery closer to the world of humans. Hermes is like the wild wind – I know him only by what he moves. He is a swift and shapeshifting god, transparent and elusive. He seems to prefer to make himself known secretly, as a pure numinous and invisible presence.[10]

How then can we genuinely get to know Hermes? For me, as a singer, it would be natural to do this through singing since songs give my soul wings. Hermes is an archetypal being, a natural born musician, and if we remember that Hermes' essence is like the wind, we might feel his presence in the very breath that carries our songs. In Greek, the word for breath is *pneuma* which also means *spirit*, and we can therefore experience Hermes as the spirit of the wind.

Hermes is a bringer of divine gifts and messages – he carries them both into the human realm and into the abode of the gods. In addition to this role, Hermes also magically retrieves things from where we did not expect to find them. If we are not prepared for change, these hermetic events can be deeply disturbing, to say the least. As an inner companion, Hermes is more of a winged *puer aeternus*, a child-god, forever young, and not the most trustworthy and consistent ally. But he is a soul guide, and this adds an unusual ancient *senex* wisdom to this eternally young god. So, for those who seek music, and for those longing for adventures, Hermes is the guide to follow – as long as we are aware that being on the musical path with Hermes will definitively have its high peaks and deep valleys.

As a donor of music, Hermes is very generous and transmits his musical knowledge willingly and without hesitation. This generosity is described in *The Hymn to Hermes*, and one example of this is in his relation to his brother Apollo to whom he gifts the lyre. Hermes is also initiated in the craft of making musical instruments, and while doing so he makes us aware that we are dependent on the realm of animals. The little tortoise was sacrificed, and her shell became the first sounding chamber. The strings were made of the guts of a lamb. In a deeper sense, Hermes' musical craft shows us that for music to be born we must tune into our instincts, and that they therefore need to be honored.[11]

"In alchemy the tortoise was regarded as the raw material for the zither which Mercury was to fashion from a tortoise-shell. The transformation of the tortoise into zither would epitomize the art of alchemy... the symbol of the Art." The shape of the tortoise is mysterious, and many religions and cultures see it as the sacred "bearer of the cosmos," in possession of the "power of prophecy."[12] C.G. Jung also said that in dreams, the tortoise can be a "theriomorphic symbol of the Self."[13]

It is an enigma how the harmonic patterns on the surface of the tortoise's shell resemble the geometric patterns (Chladni-figures), that sound frequencies create in sand on a metallic plate.[14] Music can be translated into numbers and, as Jung and von Franz write, numbers are ordering principles, archetypes of order that have become conscious. Here we have the tortoise, a bearer of the whole cosmic order, carrying musical mathematical patterns on the dome of her shell. If the tortoise is a "theriomorphic symbol of the Self," then this might mean that Hermes created the lyre out of the musical Self.

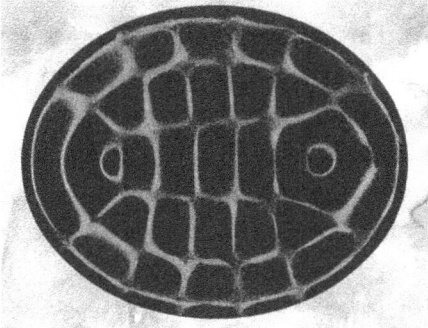
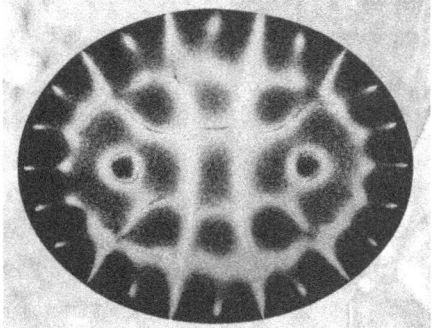

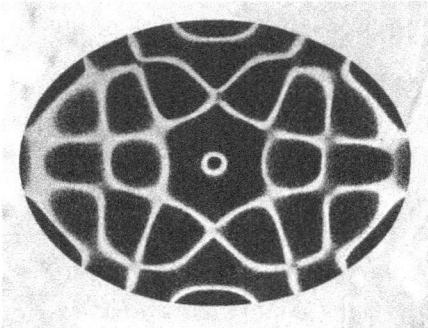
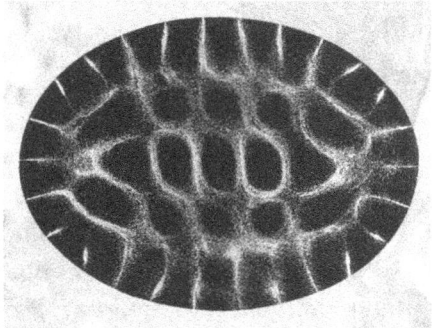

15

Today's science has shown that both humans and the whole cosmos, down to the very subatomic levels, in their essence, seem to consist of musical string patterns. Marie-Louise von Franz also writes that "oscillatory, serial and periodic phenomena are a mysterious aspect of the whole universe, appearing in waves, rotations, pulsations, turbulences and circulations. According to field theory, even each subatomic particle perpetually 'sings its song,' producing rhythmic patterns of energy." And she quotes A. Portmann: "Every form of life appears to us as a Gestalt with a specific development in time as well as space. Living things, like melodies, might be said to be configured time."[16]

Do we humans therefore resonate deeply with the vibrating harmonic Self since our souls feel that we are all basically musical compositions, irresistibly and constantly drawn towards the unfathomable, the mysterious musical magnet – the Self – the Divine conductor of it all? If so, we had better listen and tune into those grand suprasensory harmonics that wish us well. This deep tuning act of the soul might be easier in the musical company of Hermes.

Hermes, as a being, can be perceived in a wide spectrum of ways and this applies also to his dark and mysterious sides. Some scholars, for example Norman O. Brown, write about the many aspects of Hermes as a thief, and this role is also mentioned in *The Homeric Hymns, The Iliad,* and *The Odyssey*.[17] Brown elaborates extensively on this theme in *Hermes the Thief*, but makes it clear that when it comes to Hermes, we are encountering a divine and magical being who is removing something or someone "secretly." This hermetic and secret act has to do with the genius of trickery and does not necessarily mean theft or "violation of property rights." Antoine Faivre dives deeper into the theme of this mercurial act and explains:

> *"Hermes, unlike Prometheus, steals things only in order to put them back in circulation. Thus one could speak of his function as psychopomp as encompassing the 'circulation' of souls. This function is dual, for Hermes is not content merely to lead souls to the kingdom of the dead: he also goes there to find them and bring them back to the land of the living."[18]*

Jung has written extensively about Hermes/Mercurius and in his essay *The Spirit Mercurius* he writes that he is "a redeeming psychopomp, an evasive trickster, and God's reflection in physical nature."[19] In the chapter *The Psychology of the Trickster*, Jung analyses the main character traits of the subversive archetypal trickster figure and concludes that the trickster is connected with the "reversal of the hierarchic order."[20] Hermes is known for his theft of cattle from Apollo but, in the light of Jung's words, I would rather see this as a compensatory act since Hermes was Apollo's brother and the twelfth god-to-be among the Olympians. While secretly "walking backwards"[21] an archetypal way of trickster movement, and removing the cattle from Apollo's territory, Hermes reclaimed a part of what was rightfully his. Considering the famous power status of Apollo "the one who shoots from afar" it is no wonder that the trickster in Hermes wanted to bring home some of Apollo's instinctual cow power.

The interesting aspect of this adventure is that despite Hermes' longing for "meat," he never kept all the cattle for his own dinners. Instead, by night, he invented the art of fire making, in a typical swift and hermetic way, and when he had mastered the mystery of kindling fire, he sacrificed the cattle in twelve parts towards the twelve gods. The cow is in many cultures connected to the archetypal feminine. Professor Mircea Eliade even writes that "the cow is one of the epiphanies of the great mother."[22]

In the book *Animal Life in Nature*, *Myth and Dreams*, Elisabeth Caspari describes how important these rites and sacrifices of cattle were to the Greeks. "The fertility rites of the Greek goddess Hera involved the sacred marriage of the lunar cow with the solar bull, a celebration of agricultural renewal. Sacred herds of cattle were kept at her temple in Argos."[23] Hermes was not the goddess Hera's son, but a fruit of her husband Zeus' many love affairs. I will not go into any symbolical interpretations of what Hermes' sacrifice to Hera could mean, but I find it essential to remember that Hermes' secret acts of removal often have a hidden purpose which in the future could benefit both humans and gods.

The whole event with Hermes and Apollo leads to another reversal of Apollonian power – a fair share of divine gifts and roles, which Apollo willingly gives to his little brother after having been initiated into the world of music by this talented fellow. Hermes was appointed by Apollo to be the master of guidance – the *psychopompos* – the one who can cross the boundaries between the land of the living and the land of the dead. He is the messenger and soul guide to and from the underworld – the realm of Hades and Persephone.[24] In this "alliance and love" Apollo gives Hermes a golden rod and grants him "that amongst the immortals no other would be more dear, neither god nor man begotten by Zeus."

The only thing Apollo keeps for himself is the gift of prophecy, "the mind of Zeus," and does this with firmness and authority. "I alone of the gods who live for ever shall know."[25] What Apollo does share with Hermes is the oracular power of three winged sisters "who feed on combs of honey."[26] These bee nymphs resemble the Thriai – the maiden trinities who were known for their ability to interpret the signs and omens of nature while at times using mantic pebbles. There are also the Melissae – the honey priestesses who, under the influence of an intoxicant made of honey, could deliver prophecies.[27] The feminine triad can also be connected to the Moirai – the goddesses of fate, since "fate" is how they are called in the Hymn to Hermes.

Historically, the Pythian pre-Olympic priestess of Delphi remained 'the Delphic bee' long after Apollo had taken possession of the ancient oracle and shrine.[28] In this lyrical passage below it is stated by Apollo that his father "did not stop them." This is also in line with the Greek myths in which we are informed that all beings, including the immortal ones, had to submit to the Moirai – the directors of the inevitable and unturnable, the "time-measured" web and thread of life. If they are the Melissae, then perhaps it did not bother Zeus since they were the ones who fed him as a baby in the Cretan cave, where he was hiding from his father the god Chronos.

> *"For there are some Fates, three of them, sisters by birth, virgins, who take pleasure in their swift wings (and) … they taught divination independent of me, while I was still a child practising it, around my cattle. My father did not stop them. From there, they fly, now here, now there, and eat beeswax and accomplish everything. And when they have fed, on the golden honey, they are inspired."* [29]

44

In whichever way we choose to interpret the feminine triad of sisters, it is obvious that the musician Hermes is given the prophetic vision from an oracular threefold feminine principle associated with fate. Therefore, if we turn to Hermes for help in the dark, he might gift us some whispering songs on how to make the best of our fate. Hermes can see through darkness and discern the twists and turns of the winding path, long before we get to the end. However, following the musical guidance of Hermes does not necessarily mean constant luck and good fortune, since this winged guide sometimes makes detours into depths of misfortune.

As a musical Olympian god and brother of the authoritarian Apollo, it would be natural for the trickster in Hermes to question apollonian laws. I am sure the cunning side of Hermes did do this, as there might be other prophecies as accurate as "the mind of Zeus." In anchoring the role of guide in the underworld, Hermes might encounter Hecate, a goddess of liminality, and perhaps, during these dimly lit otherworldly sessions, be given information about things to come and things to leave undone. By entering the earth itself, Hermes can come face to face with the Great Mother and her serpents and this descent into the chthonic powers may give him some first-hand Dionysian premonitions, which are beyond the mission control tower of the self-appointed oracle of Apollo.

Knowing that hermetic musical prophecies emerge and rise within a different sphere than Apollo's, a source distinct from Zeus, we can expect them to be expressed in a way that resonates with their feminine Bee-sisters. The hermetic resonances of omens are likely to buzz or sting or hum around us in a winged musical dance with an outcome that can be as sweet or as sticky as honey.

The bees are important for the survival of our ecosystem, and here the prophecy of Hermes could be crucial. Jungian analyst Rafael Lopéz-Pedraza also elaborated on the difference between Apollonian and Hermetic prophecies and how Hermes' omens can manifest as somatic symptoms.

"Apollo's oracle needs an external element and gives an answer to a specific question. His oracle was in words, whereas Hermes' omens, manifest in the body, having a physiological, somatic

expression, with a feeling and emotional tone. We can risk saying that Hermes' omens have a strange connection with the neuro-vegetative system, expressing themselves with the same autonomy … a connection to a deeper strata of human nature, somewhat similar to Burkert's connection of the primitive herma to the primitive realm … Hermes' omens can come in sudden flashes, very like intuitions, in the sense of seeing through the transparence … and in their own particular way respond to a given situation, making the body react with an omen."[30]

It is written in the *Hymn to Hermes* that a "love that he could not resist took hold of Apollo at heart, and he in speech to Hermes gave voice to winged words."[31] I find this a very important passage as it describes the musical effect that Hermes' nature and wisdom has on his surroundings. It not only portrays Hermes' personality, but also describes him as a very special musician since Apollo's love is evoked by the hermetic way of singing and playing the lyre. Hermes' music was embedded with the energy of Eros. This can be interpreted as though Hermes, while performing, was deeply related to and emotionally present in the music. Karl Kerényi who writes enthusiastically about his favourite Greek god, also emphasizes Hermes' close relationship to the god Eros.[32]

"As he played the clear notes, he started in prelude to sing, and the sound of his voice was lovely – bringing to pass the immortal gods and shadowy Earth in his song, recounting how first they were born and how each obtained his share. Of all the gods he first honoured in song; Mnemosyne mother of Muses, for she was assigned Maia's son."[33]

In the above lyrical passage from the *Hymn to Hermes* we likewise find Hermes' deep alliance with the mother of the muses and goddess of memory, Mnemosyne. Under her protection he learns the art of remembrance and how song can be a keeper of memories which is a knowledge all musicians and singers need. Hermes, the fruit of a love affair between Zeus and the nymph Maia, was born in a dark cave from which he escaped on the day he was born. In Hermes' song, we are told that he, first and foremost, honours Mnemosyne who is the one who looked after him. In this perspective Hermes could be seen as a stepbrother of the Muses. As much as his mother, the nymph Maia, cares for him, he is adopted and guarded by the goddess of memory, Mnemosyne. He is also held and inspired in the musical circle of the Muses.

Guided as he is by Mnemosyne and her Muses, Hermes seems to be under the influence of the feminine more than under the masculine. It is hard to imagine Zeus taking time off from his busy love affairs and heavenly roaming instead of taking care of little Hermes. In the long run however, this might have been beneficial to Hermes' fate. As Zeus was not the dominant force in his life, Hermes was probably less caught up in the solar god's heroic ideal, a fact that suited a young god who was destined to live the life of a secret messenger between worlds and mercurial guide of souls. Kerényi also emphasizes that in Hermes' world, "fame has absolutely no part" and "Hermes' skill in the *Iliad* is strictly that of the most unheroic evasion."[34]

While reading all the stories and interpretations of the god Hermes, I have been pondering over what kind of singer and musician he could symbolize? The name of the Greek mythological singer Orpheus has kept on coming up in my mind.[35] Orpheus was a son of the muse Calliope, (her name means "beautiful voice"), and therefore she acted under the same divine musical influence as Hermes. One could say that Hermes is Orpheus' step-uncle since he was adopted by Mnemosyne. The real bond between these two figures, though, is their ancestral music line. According to the myths, Hermes gave the lyre to Apollo who in turn gave the lyre to Orpheus. Since then, the lyre has been passed on to whomever has been chosen by the gods to become a lyre player. The divine ancestral line of the lyre can be inspiring for any musician to know, i.e., having a musical talent is a gift from the gods.

In this musical and spiritual context, it is well worth to remember the shamanic and liminal motifs in the stories of Hermes and Orpheus. Both have the gift to enchant gods and humans with their music, and even the realm of animals seems to be in tune with them. Hermes and Orpheus carry within them an ancient knowledge of the healing harmonics and transformational vibrations of music and song. When depicted on mosaics or vases, we also see them in connection with the serpent – Hermes with his serpent-entwined staff, and Orpheus playing his lyre surrounded by many animals and a serpent close by.

This draws Hermes and Orpheus even closer to the archetypal image of the shaman who knows the wise ways of animals, and who can easily shapeshift into the spiritual essence of the different animal forms. Likewise, this animal aspect illuminates the quality of their music – instinctual, healing and soulful. I connect animals with soul companions. The root of the word 'animal' comes from the Latin word 'anima' which means 'soul.' Kerényi also underlines that "the Hermetic-spiritual aspect exists in friendly union with the animal-divine aspect."[36]

Hermes and Orpheus are divine voyagers into the underworld, and as guides of souls well initiated in the shamanic art of soul retrieval. Orpheus is officially mostly known for his failure in the underworld, breaking his promise to Hades, i.e., turning his gaze towards Eurydice while attempting to rescue her (or his feminine soul). However, there are other versions of this myth that tell tales of Orpheus having mastered the art of descent to and ascent from the underworld.[37]

Why the major part of the human collective, and its mainstream venues, have chosen to remember Orpheus in a negative way, i.e. as a tragedy, is a book in itself and beyond the scope of this text, but it is a fact worth keeping in mind when soulfully engaging with his numinous musical presence. In whatever way we approach Orpheus, being aware that Hermes' musical presence is within him is inspiring in any orphic voyage we embark on, especially when we try "singing the soul back home."[38]

There is another therapeutical and spiritual aspect of Hermes as a singer –his ability to "lead on." I found this expression in Jungian analyst Murray Stein's book *In Midlife* in which he elaborates on this theme in his interpretation of Hermes' role as a guide of souls.[39] According to Stein, it is important to know the difference between "leading" and "leading on" and here I find that singing can have an important hermetic role. By this I mean that Hermes, using song to guide souls through liminal space shows that songs can have a transitional function, and be beacons in dark and unknown territories. Songs can hold more archetypal energy than our words. When archetypal power enters our words, our voices start changing into reciting mode, the breath deepens, and our bodies move rhythmically. Sooner or later our spoken prayers will turn hermetically fluid and transform themselves into incantations and musical songs.

The subtle force which "leads on," that which can function as a psychic guide and bridge, is the musical and hermetic element. The song becomes a transformative container of archetypal numinous energies – a sacred vehicle for a voyage across one state of mind to another, from one departure within psyche to another point of arrival. This is most obvious when we are dealing with difficult emotional processes, as in a lament mourning the loss of a loved one, or the loss of an identity we no longer resonate with. When we enter the domain of the unspeakable, either in dark sorrow or in numinous joy, the hermetic song will lend us an invisible hand, so that we may cross the many unknown boundaries, safe with soul and held within sound.

In Greek, a mediator or guide of dreams is called 'hegetor oneiron,' and here we return to the theme of "leading on," a role that is given to Hermes. According to Jungian analyst C A Meier, the Greeks believed that the gods spoke directly to humans through dreams. Dreams were therefore treated as divine messages, that in a Jungian sense "lead us on" with their inherent purpose. In his book *Healing Dream and Ritual*, Meier also points out that Asclepios – healer and son of Apollo – really is "a successor of Hermes, who was once called the god most friendly to men." Asclepios, like Hermes, "does not heal in expectation of reward, but manifests everywhere the benevolent disposition, which is characteristic of him."[40]

We see a similar Hermes' staff, with the entwined serpents, in the hand of Asclepios, the symbol that connects both to instinctual healing and feminine chthonic powers. However, as mentioned before, Hermes is "like the wind"[41] and therefore in communion with celestial powers just as he is in alliance with the chthonic earth gods and the underworld. This unusual position, or unrestricted flux between ascent and descent, hints towards the possibility of Hermes being an older god than the Olympians. Walter F Otto is also inclined to view him this way and writes that Hermes "has properties which set him apart from the circle of the children of Zeus and which, when they are closely examined, appear to be a different and older conception of deity."[42] Otto is of the same mind as Kerényi who writes that Hermes' "ithyphallic nature and as guide of souls," links him to the even more ancient Cabeiri mysteries. Hermes, according to Kerényi, has a close connection to the chthonic earth goddesses such as Hecate, to mention one.[43].

This transformation of the archetypal image of Hermes is also visible in the way he has been depicted over the past few thousand years, from phallic stone sculptures to transparent postmodern angels in computer games. The earliest symbols of Hermes were heaps of stones (Greek: *herma*), similar to the prayer stones one can find in the high mountain passes of Tibet. While travelling in the Tibetan Trans Himalayas in the summer of 1991, I was told by my Tibetan guide, that these piles of stones "are sacred points, holy Buddhist markers, which while chanting prayers can create a descent of grace so that one can ascend higher and higher." By placing another stone on this altar before heading on, one enters a cosmic and communal ritual, in resonance with all other pilgrims that have passed that way before. By the very placement of a simple hermetic stone, a stone that can 'lead on,' one is humbly asking to be granted grace on the journey that lies ahead.[44]

There is a similar description in Martin Nilsson's book *Greek Folk Religion* of how Greek peasants related and venerated the stone heaps.[45] I believe that the Greek herm-stones resonate with the Tibetan mountain stones, and with holy heaps of stones all over the planet. It is a paradoxical hermetic phenomenon that the swiftest air god of them all lives and dwells within a stone. However, many of these heaps of stones have anthropomorphic qualities. In the German and Dutch languages, a 'cairn' is known as 'Steinmann,' among the Inuits they represent an Inunguak (imitation of a figure), and in the Italian alps we find the Ometto (small man).[46]

So, what is a stone? It can mark boundaries, entrances, passageways, and the graves of those who have died. In the alchemical perspective, a stone can also be an elixir of life. I found an interesting amplification of both stone and the "cosmic Hermes" in von Franz' book, where she notes that there existed a "Hermes religion of late antiquity." She also refers to the alchemical tradition where the stone signifies "the resurrected body."[47]

The musical Hermes within the stone, the god who "leads on" as a symbolic re-surrector of soma (and therefore psyche if we perceive them as a whole), is in harmonic resonance with all journeys into liminality. They encompass a rite of passage in which there is always the expected point of resurrection. The journey is a pilgrimage and a sacrifice, the stone an offering, be it in a high mountain pass or in a valley so deep that only godly grace can grant us an ascent.

The apocryphal logion says: "lift a stone and you will find me there," and we know from the Bible that the stone was rolled away from the burial chamber, and Christ was resurrected. We also know that Christ was depicted as the Good Shepherd and that Hermes was appointed the lord of the Shepherds by Apollo. I never intended to write about Hermes and how he seems to resonate with Christ, but now, in hindsight, I see that both merge as facets of the grand archetype of the Self.

Jung suggests that the figure of Hermes/Mercurius has a complementary function to the figure of Christ, that Hermes' dim lunar and starry light of the night embodies the same mysterious guiding quality as the solar bright daylight of Christ. Jung holds up a warning hand if we ignore the hermetic light and means that we can see Hermes' guidance as instinctual wisdom of the mercurial unconscious, and Christ's light as the guidance of the conscious.

"The figure of Christ the Logos has raised the 'anima rationalis' in man to a level of importance which remains unobjectionable so long as it knows itself to be below and subject to the 'kúrios,' the Lord of Spirits. Reason, however, has set itself free and proclaimed itself the ruler… (and) Hesitantly, as in a dream, the introspective brooding of the centuries gradually put together the figure Mercurius and created a symbol which, according to all the psychological rules, stands in a compensatory relation to Christ. It

is not meant to take its place, nor is it identical with him, for then indeed it could replace him. It owes its existence to the law of compensation, and its object is to throw a bridge across the abyss separating the two psychological worlds by presenting a subtle compensatory counterpoint to the Christ image."[48]

For now, I will leave Hermes here at the crossroads, exactly where I found him, or rather where he seized my soul some thousand songs ago. I will honor him with a beautiful quote, which is originally, according to von Franz, connected to the "agatho-daimon" – the inner companion.[49]

I feel these words are in tune with Hermes, the winged messenger and guide of souls, and I hope he will reappear at some musical crossroad further down the singing line.

Looking back at what moved me most during this journey with Hermes, I felt unconditional gentleness emanating from his heart, a love he shared without expecting anything in return. Hermes seems somewhat indifferent to what I write about him, but he does take pleasure in some of my songs. I suppose this is what one could expect from a musical god who can change his shape at will, who can slip through keyholes as though it is the most natural and musical move in the world to do.

The more I read about the ways of the gods, the more they seem to temporally lend themselves – and their numinous energies – to the psyche that is trying to speak the unspeakable. When the opus is written, the songs composed, the gods move on. This, of course, is just a singer's and a woman's reflection on her journey with Hermes, a masculine musical soul companion. Hermes was, and still is, like the wind. I know and feel him the closest when I sing.

"He will come to you everywhere on your way through life
and he will reveal himself everywhere,
where and when you least expect him.
Waking, sleeping, at sea, in the street,
at night, by day
when you speak or when you are silent,
since there is nothing which he is not"

ENDNOTES

[1] Carl Gustav Jung, *Alchemical Studies*, Collected Works Vol. 13, Princeton University Press 1983, p. 230. Jung quotes the Erythraen Sibyl speaking about Hermes.

[2] Temenos: Greek for inner sanctuary.

[3] For more information on shamanism and the ancient sacred traditions of Greece see Peter Kingsley, *In the Dark Places of Wisdom,* The Golden Sufi Center, 2010 and E R Dodds, *The Greeks and the Irrational*, University of California Press, 1951.

[4] For more information about Lena Måndotter's film about Orpheus, *Letters to a Young Singer* and all other artistic and song-therapeutic work visit www.lenamandotter.com

[5] Carl Gustav Jung, ed. Aniela Jaffé, *Memories, Dreams, Reflections*, Vintage Books/ Random House, 1989, p. 183.

[6] Henry Corbin, *Swedenborg and Esoteric Islam,* Swedenborg Foundation, 2014, pp. 1 - 33.

[7] Antoine Faivre, *The Eternal Hermes – from Greek God to Alchemical Magus*, Phanes Press, 1995, p. 65.

[8] Gaston Bachelard, *On Poetic Imagination and Reverie*, Spring Publications, 2014.

[9] Henry Corbin, *Spiritual Body and Celestial Earth*, p. XII. Here Corbin uses the concept of 'tawil' i.e. "to reconduct something to its source, to its archetype, to its true reality."

[10] German mythographer W.H. Rosher "identified Hermes as the wind" and from this identity of a wind-god, he then tied all the most known hermetic functions: swift, winged, inventor of the lyra, thief, guide of souls, messenger etc. Source: Murray Stein, *The Principle of Individuation*, Chiron Publications, 2006, p. 144.

[11] *The Homeric Hymns*, "Hymn to Hermes" nr 4 and nr 18, Oxford University Press, 2008, pp. 43 - 64 and p. 82.

[12] Jean Chevalier & Alain Gheerbrant, *Dictionary of Symbols*, p. 1016.

[13] Ad De Vries & Arthur de Vries, *Elsevier's Dictionary of Symbols*, Emerald Group Publishing, 2009, p. 523.

[14] Alexander Lauterwasser, *Water Sound Images*, MACROmedia Publishing, p. 62. (Ernst Chladni lived 1756 - 1827).

[15] Photograph by Alexander Lauterwasser, Tortoise/Chladni-figures, *Water Sound Images*, p. 62. MACROmedia Publishing, www.cymaticsource.com

[16] Marie Louise von Franz, *Time – Rhythm and Repose*, Thames & Hudson, 1978, reprint 1992, p. 51.

[17] Norman O. Brown, *Hermes the Thief – The Evolution of a Myth*, Random House, 1969, p. 10.

[18] Antoine Faivre, *The Eternal Hermes – from Greek God to Alchemical Magus*, Phanes Press, 1995, p. 14.

[19] Carl Gustav Jung, *Alchemical Studies*, Collected Works Vol. 13, Princeton University Press, 1983, 3rd print, p. 237.

[20] Paul Radin, *The Trickster – A Study in American Indian Mythology*, (commentaries by Carl Gustav Jung and Karl Kerényi), Schocken Books, p. 195.

[21] *The Homeric Hymns*, p. 45.

[22] Mircea Eliade, *Rites and Symbols of Initiation*, Spring Publications, 2009, p. 99.

[23] Elizabeth Caspari, *Animal Life in Nature, Myth and Dreams*, Chiron Publications, p. 63.

[24] Karl Kerényi, *Hermes – Guide of Souls*, Spring Publications, 2009.

[25] Karl Kerényi, *Hermes – Guide of Souls*, Spring Publications, 2009.

[26] Ibid., p. 63.

[27] https://en.wikipedia.org/wiki/Thriae

[28] https://en.wikipedia.org/wiki/Hyria_(Boeotia There is also an interesting connotation of the archaic Greek word "Hyria" which could mean "sisters of the bee-hive" and in Cretan 'hyron' means 'swarm of bees' or 'bee-hive.'

[29] Karl Kerényi, *Hermes – Guide of Souls*, p. 63.

[30] Rafael Lopéz-Pedraza, *Hermes and His Children*, Daimon Verlag, 2010, p. 70.

[31] Ibid., p. 58.

[32] Carl Gustav Jung and Karl Kerényi, *Essays on a Science of Mythology*, Princeton University Press, 1969, p. 53.

[33] *The Homeric Hymns*, p. 58.

[34] Karl Kerényi, *Hermes – Guide of Souls*, p. 27.

[35] Lena Måndotter, music performance, *Orpheus – do not turn around*, Malmö Arthall, Sweden, 2004 and film *Letters to a Young Singer*, 2008, www.lenamandotter.com

[36] Karl Kerényi, *Hermes – Guide of Soul* p. 109.

[37] *The Mysteries – Papers from the Eranos Yearbooks*, ed. Joseph Campbell, Bollingen Series XXX Vol.2, Princeton University Press, 1990, p. 68, (Walter Wili "The Orphic Mysteries and the Greek Spirit"). See also W.K.C. Guthrie, *Orpheus and Greek Religion*, Princeton University Press, original print 1952, paperback print 1993, p. 31, Ann Wroe, *Orpheus – the Song of Life*, Pimlico, 2012, Algis Uzdavinys, *Orpheus and the Roots of Platonism*, The Matheson Trust, 2011, p. 41, and Gianfranco Salvatore, *Orpheus before Orpheus -The Myth of the Magic Citharode*, in Spring Journal, "Orpheus". Vol 71, Spring – A Journal of Archetype and Culture, 2004, p. 171 - 191.

[38] Caitlín Mathews, *Singing the Soul Back Home*, Element Books, 1996.

[39] Murray Stein, *In Midlife – a Jungian Perspective*, Spring Publ., 2009. We can also find the role of 'leading on' the ghosts in the Odyssey where "Hermes the Healer led them on [—-] to the fields of asphodel, where the dead, the burnt-out wraths of mortals, make their home." (See Kerényi p. 29).

[40] C.A. Meier, *Healing Dream and Ritual*, Daimon Verlag, 2009, pp. 104 and 112.

[41] Murray Stein, *The Principle of Individuation*, Chiron Publications, 2006, p. 144.

[42] Walter F. Otto, *The Homeric Gods – the Spiritual Significance of Greek Religion*, Thames and Hudson, 1979, p. 104.

[43] Karl Kerényi, *Hermes – Guide of Souls*, p. 95.

[44] A journey in Tibet, from the city of Lhasa across the Trans Himalayas where I joined the Tibetan pilgrims to circumambulate their sacred

mountain Kailash in the summer of 1991. See also book: *Där Alla Änglar Fallit (Where All Angels Have Fallen)*, Art Distribution, 1992.

[45] Murray Stein, *The Principle of Individuation*, p. 147.

[46] https://en.wikipedia.org/wiki/Cairn

[47] Marie-Louise von Franz, *Projection and Re-collection in Jungian Psychology*, Open Court Publ., 1995, pp. 143 - 159.

[48] Carl Gustav Jung, *Alchemical Studies*, Collected Works Vol. 13, pp. 244 - 245.

[49] Marie-Louise von Franz, *Projection and Re-collection in Jungian Psychology*, p. 151.

CHAPTER IV
Serpent On The Soul's Horizon

"It often happens that one fears what has to be,
what in the deepest sense belongs to one.
One fears it, and yet one wants it at the same time.
One should really press the fear to one's heart and say:
'This is, after all, precisely what I want.' C.G. JUNG[1]

Serpent Resonance

To embrace and hold the numinous opposites is a psychic art and a musical skill perhaps not meant to master, but to humbly aim and pray for. After having journeyed on the wings of Hermes and other musical spirits in the whirling high winds, I would now like to land with both feet on the ground. This could be seen as a musical counterpoint, a balancing complimentary act, a deep descent after having ascended to the heights. These vertical movements depend on each other and within them there are points of tension and centers of harmony.

The musical secret of ascent and descent seems to be known by Hermes since he always navigates the many directions of the universe, carrying his magic rod with the spiraling serpent. Why is this serpent of the deep earth so important to a musical god of the high skies? And why is it that the Greek mythological figures, master musician Orpheus and the master healer Asclepios, also appear in the company of the serpent? Like Hermes, both Orpheus and Asclepios performed their healing rituals with music as a profound and sacred part for transformation to take place.[2] Is there a mysterious liminal link, a primordial vibrating resonance between the serpent and the world of music?

The serpent is in many myths a divine instinctual messenger, and I will relate this to some song-therapeutic and spiritual aspects of singing. The serpent knows the art of shedding its skin and how to renew itself. In many shamanic cultures the serpent is honored and seen as a powerful initiator of transformation – of death, rebirth, and resurrection.[3] There is a mystery and ambiguity around the serpent, a symbolic charge that can bring animated energy to the soul and therefore into the song. Jung wrote that when the images of animals disappear from the symbols of religions, it symbolizes the end of religion. What deep knowledge do the four-legged ones, the winged ones and the winding ones that inhabit our planet have, that we humans need to honor and protect?

Serpent as Symbol

"What has struck me, again and again, is how close auditory energy is to psychic energy… Since sound is mostly experienced as a flow of energy, as a force, it is always elusive, just like psychic energy… Auditory energy is both powerful and subtle. Uniquely expressive, it vibrates us to the core."[4]

The way of the serpent is an eternal spiraling way, and just like sound, a flowing and rolling energetic force. Only another serpent can deeply understand this way of rising and rolling across the soils and sands of this Earth. It requires a specific instinctive perception and art of listening to understand the rhythmical movements and high-pitched hissing sounds of the serpent. It is purely instinctual and in tune with the Anima Mundi.

Before musically embarking on this journey into the serpent's world, I would like to define the way I use and interpret the word 'symbol.' Therefore, I open this text with some voices within the field of Jungian analytical psychology about symbols and archetypes.

One can relate to a symbol as something that will always transcend itself, and it can originate from the imaginal realm and the unconscious.

The many inherent meanings of a symbol are endless and often very difficult, sometimes impossible, for our rational and cognitive understanding to interpret. In my own work with song therapy, I can become aware of how a symbol sometimes calls upon another symbol, and *not* an interpretation, before it reveals its deepest depths. In practice this means that a song is asking for another song, a sound calls for another sound or change of timbre to make itself known before it discloses its psychic messages.

In a practical musical situation, I can sing the old Hebrew hymn "Avinu Malkeinu" and feel all that this song evokes not only in me as the singer, but also in the audience as listeners and witnesses. Instead of analyzing and talking this song to pieces after I have sung it, and trying to find out what it symbolically holds and means, I can instead follow it with another old Hebrew song "Shir Lama 'Alot."[5] By doing this, the songs will resonate and illuminate each other and by the combination of these two songs a third arises – a realization of a transcendent meaning.

This does not mean there is necessarily something wrong in using our thinking function and conscious cognitive understanding. The example above is just another way of resonating with a theme or image. This way of resonating could perhaps be called the feminine way, just like the way of animals – like sounding serpents in the sand do or when wolves reach communal understanding when one after the other joins in the moonlit howling choir. It means something deep – as deep as the night – way beyond the stars.

Being in this "acoustic vessel"[6] and resonating around a symbol, instead of explicitly talking in detail, is a way of pending and still moving forward, not in a straight line, but instead sidewinding in a more serpentine way. In song therapy one can also use this technique when dealing with verbally or cognitively handicapped people or clients suffering from autism, stroke and similar symptoms. The therapist and the client sound each other – in and out and around and beyond. Doing this awakens slumbering instincts in the client.

An important aspect of a symbol is that it is only alive if it carries inherent meaning. There comes a time however when these meanings are no longer there, and we must admit that the symbol is emptied of numinous energy – at least for now – and has turned into a mere sign. In the therapeutic song-temenos one can experience how one symbol dies and dissolves into the arms of another – alive the new one rises out of the vast musical reservoir of the unconscious. The psychic energy manifests itself in a series of symbols, and behind these schemes of images there is an inherent and instinctual force that calls for an increase of consciousness in the whole psychic and musical process. Murray Stein writes that "the psyche has a forward-moving and creative function, and when symbols become activated, they serve to organize the structures and patterns that libido follows."[7]

Jung wrote that symbols were the bridges that brought him across into the luminous landscape of the unconscious. This psychic journey is visually depicted in *The Red Book* and its many shades of meanings distilled in his biographical book *Memories, Dreams, Reflections*.[8] Symbols were of greatest value when he worked with schizophrenic patients and this work made him aware of the sounds, voices, and images of the psychoid world. A central theme for Jung is the symbol's subjective meaning for each individual, but also how symbols are imaginal manifestations of the archetypes which reside in the collective unconscious.

"A symbol always presupposes that the chosen expression is the best possible description or formulation of a relatively unknown fact, which is none the less known to exist or is postulated as existing… So long as the symbol is a living thing, it is an expression for something that cannot be characterized in any other or better way. The symbol is alive only so long as it is pregnant with meaning. But once its meaning has been borne out of it, once that expression is found which formulates the thing sought, expected or divined even better hitherto accepted symbol, then the symbol is dead. … every psychological expression is a symbol if we assume that it states or signifies something more and other than itself which eludes our present knowledge. …

Whether a thing is a symbol or not depends chiefly on the attitude of the observing consciousness; for instance, on whether it regards a given fact not merely as such but also as an expression of something unknown."[9]

It is by getting to know the many meanings of symbols with all our functions – feeling, intuition, thinking and sensing that we are made aware of the archetypes and therefore also of ourselves and the many prisms of the Self. Since archetypes are configurations or "systems of psychic energy" we cannot experience an archetype directly.[10] Instead the archetypal and psychic energy must come through a medium, be it image or sound, before it makes itself known. Jungian analyst Brigitte Egger also refers to von Franz and imagines the energy of the archetype as though passing through a veil, or a membrane, between the unconscious and the conscious. At the exact point where this passing through takes place, the archetype transforms itself into a symbol or a series of symbols – in dreams, active imaginations, songs, or other creative processes.[11]

Stein describes the symbol as a "psychic transformer" and refers to the transformation of libido, which from the Jungian view means psychic energy. He emphasizes that "symbols transform libido in an 'upward' direction,"[12] i.e. towards a conscious attitude which can embrace the whole spectrum and stratum of polarizing forces – the totality of the psyche where instinct is aligned with body, mind and soul.

The numinous power which the symbol carries, and how this numen stems from the archetype, is important. The numinous aspect of the symbol is therefore something that makes it stand apart from a metaphor which is created by human consciousness. The metaphor might not hint towards the archetypal world in the same numinous way as a symbol does. A symbol seems to have a deeper *duende*. We can be fascinated by the paradoxical nature of metaphors, but perhaps not touched and lifted by the same seizing force that the magnetic archetypal symbols have.

Tuning into the Serpent

The human projections into the world of serpents are immense and we tend to read in much more than there can possibly be in these creatures. From a reductive perspective the serpent is a crawling predator on the surface of the earth, potentially dangerous, possibly phallic and very powerful. That is however a somewhat detached and limited perspective. Since animals frequently appear in our dreams and fantasies the unconscious obviously considers them to be of great importance to our psychic creative processes and our individuation journey. There is more soul to animals than the ego can see. We would not call them *animals* if it were not so. We use the word for soul (latin: anima) when we name them, and this conveys a soulful depth that perhaps only our own human animal soul can reach.

If we ignore an animal symbol, "it will still function within us and will possess us inevitably without our knowledge" writes Jungian analyst Barbara Hannah.[13] Aniela Jaffé, also a Jungian analyst, stresses that the return of our life vitality depends on our ability to really relate to an animal when it turns up in our dreams. There will be no transformation of libido to a higher consciousness with just an intellectual understanding of an animal symbol. The image needs to enter deep into the body and all our four functions need to be active in this psychic process:

> *"The familiar dream in which the dreamer is pursued by an animal nearly always indicates that an instinct has been split off from consciousness and ought to be (or is trying to be) readmitted or integrated into life. The more dangerous the behaviour of the animal in the dream, the more unconscious is the primitive and instinctual soul of the dreamer, and the more imperative is its integration into his life if some irreparable evil is to be forestalled."*[14]

Marie-Louise von Franz says the serpent's "image oscillates between beneficence and malevolence"[15] The serpent often embraces the two opposites simultaneously, as described in the biblical story about the garden of Eden where the serpent, in relationship to Eve, functions as the tempter, but also as the initiator to becoming conscious. The serpent is related to gaining another kind of knowledge – the wisdom of the forbidden fruit, and this can only be gained by losing one's innocence and paradisical illusions. The image of the forbidden fruit can be very useful when working with clients who are insecure of their voice and their ability to sing. Singing can for some people feel as though they are entering a forbidden realm, a dangerous territory. Especially vulnerable are those who have had their singing voices shamed by unconscious parents and judgmental teachers and authorities.[16]

The serpent appears in many stories and myths. In *The Brother Grimm's Fairytales* there is one tale called "The White Snake."[17] In this tale the serpent is once again the initiator of a servant's way to independence and individuation. This is a common motif, i.e., by tasting the forbidden, in this case a bit of the serpent, the servant suddenly understands the language of animals. In other words, he has connected with his instincts and with a world that was closed to him before and "therefore held off in the unconscious."[18]

What is also important in this tale is that the knowledge gained, originates from a real experience in life, not by any intellectual under-standing from books. To individuate away from repressive authorities, one needs to stick one's teeth into the snake, have a good but modest bite and really digest and integrate the nourishment of the serpent meal. That is a totally different story of individuation than just checking the snake's possible meanings in symbol dictionaries.

Stein also distinguishes between the divine revelation by the serpent and "the light of revelation from above … where the spirit comes from above and not from below." The serpent's knowledge is a "profound initiation into the language of the instinctual psyche." He refers to Paracelsus who called this wisdom "the *lumen naturae*, the light of nature" and describes it as "a state of grace."[19]

Hannah structures her interpretation of the archetypal symbolism of the serpent under different functions which also shows its symbolical ambiguity. The serpent as "demon of the earth, darkness and evil … as spirit of light and wisdom … as the Ouroboros of cyclic life … as a symbol of ghosts and renewal … as union of opposites and communication of the divine."[20]

The serpent behaves in ways similar to our own unconscious. That is, the serpent can be totally invisible or still as a dead stick, and then suddenly come alive or appear from nowhere and in one split second unexpectedly strike. These kinds of surprising moves are also typical for how the images and symbols in dreams behave. This striking quality is present when they overtake us unprepared and create within us an overwhelming terror of the unknown.

When working therapeutically and artistically with our voices and songs we can also feel struck by sounds that seem to come from the unknown, from dark psychic depths, from a realm totally *Other*. In these situations, people often feel that the sound they gave voice to was not them, it was someone else, i.e. the sound emerged from outside their ego's comfort zone. New vocal sounds therefore often take time to integrate into their personal lives – and into their songs. The time this takes should be nourished and respected.

The serpent is also in possession of a profound prophetic talent which was known by the oracle of Delphi. This oracular serpent power is later reclaimed by the musical god Apollo. Some sacred music also shares this similar prophetic element. Corbin writes that "Only musical incantation can make us feel and sometimes see it, inasmuch as listening to music has the power to suddenly render one *clairvoyant*."[21] The prophetic energy of song was also widely used in the old Nordic religions and was part of the song practice of the *seidr*. The prophecies were sung and rhythmically recited in a meandering serpentine way as for example in the old Voluspa prophecy. It tells the story of the creation of the world, its coming end and its subsequent rebirth.

Jung points to the three main roles of the serpent as "earth daimon," "savior" and "time symbol." Music exists in time and is also deeply related to the daimonic and to the saviour. One common aspect in the serpent's role as saviour and bearer of wisdom is its multiple shining and hypnotizing eyes. Marie-Louise von Franz concludes that the "multiplicity of eyes may be connected with the multiplicity of subliminal perceptions:

man is so to speak, more clear-sighted in the unconscious than in the conscious, and, above all, sees into many more directions simultaneously. Hence the serpent's power of prediction."[22]

The deep fear of the serpent can be compared to the deep fear of singing. From my own experience, it is important to give clients time to work through their fear since we are dealing with this chthonic Other. As I wrote earlier, a song can also be felt and perceived as an unknown being. There is usually an initial phase of fear which slowly become bearable. Further on in the process one can acquaint oneself with and have a closer feel of the serpent within the song. I have also confronted the serpent, in dreams and in song, where it was of utmost importance to take hold of it by the neck and press the poison out of its fangs. By doing this the poison was transformed into medicine – a medicine that became a cure both on a physical and on a psychological level.

In the *Nietzsche Zarathustra Seminars*, Jung takes a close look at the serpent's pure physical characteristics, describing how the serpent represents the lower nerve system, i.e. the sympathetic nervous system which rules over all the important centers of the body. We should therefore pay close attention, so we do not deviate from our instinctual serpent roots. Jung even goes as far as saying that ignoring the serpent's animal instinct can under certain circumstances lead to one's own death.[23] Both von Franz and Jung have also expressed that people who are born artists should not ignore their destiny since by ignoring and blocking these creative powers can cause severe physical and psychic symptoms. Personally, I can only confirm that if I do not sing every day, I quickly lose the deep resonance with my life path. It is as if surrendering to the creative power of the serpent is the only way I can stay in tune with the creative forces in my life.

Some serpents can swallow beings who are much bigger than themselves. This shows that the serpent has a very patient and persistent side which enables it to digest what seems indigestible. All psychic processes call for periods of integration. Reclaiming one's soul songs definitively consists of digestion of new psychospiritual musical knowledge. It is not uncommon for us to sometimes feel that we do not have (or do not deserve) the capacity to digest, to incorporate and truly live our new musical soul life. Perhaps it is then time for us to call on the serpent's wisdom on how to take it all in, how to fathom the power of the song, so that it may be used as serene musical nourishment for body, heart, and soul.

The serpent has a highly sensitive nervous system. It senses the rhythms, vibrations and sounds of other animals in its surroundings by laying its head on the surface of the earth. It can also detect ultraviolet light of urine tracks left by animals that have passed by. Furthermore, it has ingenious detectors that can see and feel body heat. With its forked tongue the serpent can also smell in stereo and accurately sense who is where and who is doing what.

The serpent orients itself by a sense of seeing and hearing, and ways of moving that are not typical for us humans. Having watched Jungian analyst and film director Peter Ammann's film about San (African bushmen) recently, I truly believe that those earthbound people would have an easier time than urbanized people to tune into the frequency of the spirit of the serpent.[24] The art of tuning into this chthonic wisdom seems to depend on how low we are willing to bow and how close to the ground we are prepared to put our ears. Music is all about deep, deep listening.

In shamanic cultures shapeshifting is a way of transforming oneself into a guardian animal to receive its wisdom. Perhaps we can learn from this ancient spiritual technique when singing and working with symbols. It is "a technique of ecstasy."[25] The shaman does not shapeshift into a specific serpent that he has seen in a cave. The shaman sings and shapeshifts into the essence of the universal soul and body of the serpent and enters its spiraling serpentism. By so doing the shaman acquires the wisdom and skills of the sacred serpent.

Jung wrote that when we listen to the serpent we learn about "sympathy" since the serpent symbolically represents the sympathetic nervous system. In the world of song, sympathy is at its core and imperative for mutual musical resonance. Therefore, we must always wait for a sign of agreement from our inner serpent before we make any final musical decisions. The serpent's answer usually comes to us in dreams, visions, or hypnagogic states. Sympathy for Jung also meant the ability to become one with the Anima Mundi which he locates in the collective unconscious and therefore in the human body.

> *"Our unconscious is surely located in the body, and you mustn't think this is a contradiction to the statement I usually make, that the unconscious is everywhere; for if you could put yourself into your sympathetic system, you would know what sympathy is – you would understand why the nervous system is called sympathetic. You would then feel that you were in everything, you would not feel yourself as an isolated being, would not experience the world and life as your own private experience – as we most certainly do inasmuch as we are conscious persons. In the sympathetic system you would experience not as a person but as mankind, or even as belonging to the animal kingdom, you would experience nothing in particular, but the whole phenomena of life as if it were one … and you must necessarily assume that such awareness would be without time … the sympathetic system needs no time; it is at the same time everywhere … the sympathetic nervous system of the body is the organ by which you have the possibility of such an awareness, therefore you can say the collective unconscious is in the lower centres of the brain and the spinal cord and the sympathetic system."*[26]

Many find the serpent distant from our human realm and "un-sympathetic," and most of us fear this reptile's presence. Paradoxically the serpent is the one who can teach us about what we consciously least associate it with – sympathy. Sympathy is a way of empathically and acutely resonating with our surroundings which is crucial if we are to be in tune with the world of music.

ENDNOTES

[1] Carl Gustav Jung, *Children's Dreams – notes from the seminar given in 1936 - 1940*, Princeton University Press, p. 263.

[2] C.A. Meier, *Healing Dream and Ritual – Ancient Incubation and Modern Psychotherapy*, Daimon Verlag, 2009 (fourth ed.) p. 73.

[3] Joseph Henderson and Maud Oakes, *The Wisdom of the Serpent*, Princeton University Press, 1990.

[4] Mary Lynn Kittelson, *Sounding the Soul*, pp. 274 - 276.

[5] Lena Måndotter, music albums *Songs from the River*, Rootsy/Warner Music (2008), *Live at the Cathedral* (2015) and *Prayers & Prophecies – Live at the Palladium*, Kameleont Production (2017).

[6] Mary Lynn Kittelson, *Sounding the Soul*, p. 121.

[7] *The Symbolic Life*, ed. Nancy Cater & Murray Stein, Spring – a journal of Archetype and Culture, 2009, p. 6.

[8] Carl Gustav Jung, *The Red Book* and Carl Gustav Jung/Aniela Jaffé, *Memories, Dreams, Reflections*, Fontana Press, 1995.

[9] Carl Gustav Jung, *Psychological Types*, Collected Works Vol. 6, Bollingen Foundation, § 814 and § 816.

[10] Marie-Louise von Franz, *Psyche and Matter*, Shambhala Publications, 1982, p. 244.

[11] Brigitte Egger, seminar series on *Synchronicity*, ISAP Zürich, November 2011.

[12] Murray Stein, *The Symbolic Life*, p. 7.

[13] Barbara Hannah, *The Archetypal Symbolism of Animals*, Chiron Publications, 2006, p. IX.

[14] Aniela Jaffé's chapter in Carl Gustav Jung's, *Man and His Symbols*, Dell Publishing 1968, p. 236.

Endnotes

[15] Marie-Louise von Franz, *The Cat – a Tale of Feminine Redemption*, Inner City Books, 1999, p. 55.

[16] For further expansion on the theme of shame see also Mario Jacoby, *Shame and the Origins of Self-Esteem*.

[17] Jacob and Wilhelm Grimm, *The Complete Grimm's Fairytales*, Pantheon Books, 1944/1972, pp. 98 - 101.

[18] Murray Stein, *The Principle of Individuation*, p. 70.

[19] Ibid., p. 73.

[20] Barbara Hannah, *The Archetypal Symbolism of Animals*, p. 5.

[21] Henry Corbin, *The Voyage and the Messenger*, North Atlantic Books, 1998, p. 233.

[22] Carl Gustav Jung, *Children's Dreams*, *Notes from the seminar given in 1936 - 1940*, Princeton University Press, 2006, pp. 240 - 263.

[23] Carl Gustav Jung, *Nietzsche Zarathustra seminar Vol. 1*, Princeton University Press, 1988, pp. 174 - 175 and pp. 750 - 751.

[24] Peter Ammann's film *The Spirit of the Rocks*.

[25] Mircea Eliade, *Shamanism – Archaic Techniques of Ecstasy*, Arkana, 1989.

[26] Carl Gustav Jung, *Nietzsche's Zarathustra Seminar Vol. 1*, pp. 174 - 175.

CHAPTER V
Musical Mirror Neurons

"Very often deeply damaged people reach for something musical in the therapist and hope that the latter will respond to something deeply musical in themselves."[1]

Recent findings in neuroscience about mirror neurons in our brain show that they function by mirroring the behavior of the other person, and thereby acting synchronistically with the other person's mirror neurons. The mirror neurons function without us being consciously aware of it in the same way our sympathetic nervous system does. This could be compared to how the serpent resonates with its surrounding environment. The ability of mirror neurons to identify with other people's mirror neurons could be seen as a temporary and fruitful *participation mystique*. This enables and increases our ability to feel both sympathy and empathy for the world around us. It is an ancient way of gaining knowledge by becoming one with the other.

The mirror neurons are created in the child's brain before the age of one. The child's growth and strength seem to depend on the consistency and availability of the outer parental mirror – the caretakers' mirror neurons, and how their sympathetic feelings transmit into the child's brain. Jungian analyst Margaret Wilkinson has published books on this topic in which she describes the mind-brain relationship from a Jungian clinical perspective. Wilkinson focuses on "the affect-regulating, relational aspects of therapy that forge new neural pathways through emotional connection, forming the emotional scaffolding that permits the development of mind."[2]

The neuroscientific theories of mirror neurons and Jung's understanding of the many shades of meanings of sympathy also resembles Mario Jacoby's theories of the therapeutic importance of 'empathy.' This empathic attitude has a similar instinctive and emotional connection – to be one and resonate with the oneness, and through this resonance to become aware of the musical mirror and vibrating resonance between the client and of oneself. The sympathy, the empathic resonance itself, is a major part of the healing process, according to Jacoby.[3]

It appears there is some psychic essence that can be transmitted in the non-verbal field. Some musicians pick up the vibrations between each other while playing and feel a mutual exchange of mysterious energies. After the concert they often have a sense of deeper knowing and connection, a sense of soul mirroring in a secret musical world. A deep heart connection between two beings seems to strengthen this mirroring, a kind of singing flow in harmonic convergence.

The music of some musicians can change you forever without them having said a word. You enter their musical field and absorb the vibrations, and when you leave their psychic field, you are transformed and have become an Other. A musical numinous mana energy touches you and its magical shimmering light envelops your soul. It is a transforming reverberation, the mirroring power of music. Being held in the arms of soulful music is very enchanting. I believe both Hermes and Eros are divine active agents in these kinds of magical musical experiences.

Wilkinson writes about the forging of new neural pathways in the brain through emotional connection. I believe it is not only neural paths that are forged, but also cardial paths, though the paths of the heart are mysterious. We enter the musical field, we take some mirroring tonal and harmonic essence to heart, and if there is true love in the song, we will never be the same. Through the musical mirror, and its vibrating power, we can cross the boundary into the realm of the Divine. This transcendent move is proof of the transition to one of the holiest dimensions of music and song.

ENDNOTES

[1] *Music and Psyche, contemporary psychoanalytic explorations"*, ed. P W Ashton & S Bloch, quote by psychoanalyst Michael Eigen, Spring Journal Books, 2010 p. 161.

[2] Margaret Wilkinson, *Coming into Mind*, Routledge, 2009, p. 2.

[3] Mario Jacoby's lectures *The Wounded Healer*, C.G. Jung Institut in Küsnacht (summer 2000) and ISAP International School of Analytical Psychology Zürich. (Autumn 2010)

CHAPTER VI
Archetypal Music Healers

Chiron, Asclepios, and Instinctual Musical Empathy

"Thus the singing creature expresses itself in and for its world. In expressing itself it becomes happily aware of the world, it cries out and joyfully lays claim to the world. The lark rises to dizzy heights in the column of air that is its world; without other purpose, it sings the song of itself and its world … A living knowledge rings in the song."[1]

Jungian psychoanalyst Mario Jacoby was a classically trained violinist who often lectured on *The Wounded Healer* including amplifications of the serpent's healing role in the Greek myths. The medicinal god Asclepios, son of Apollo, was always surrounded by serpents, if not hissing with raised heads in the forefront, then quietly present in the background of the healing process. To add more animal instinct to the situation, Asclepios was also guided by the centaur Chiron, the half god and half horse, often seen in the company of dogs. According to Kerényi, Chiron was the master instructor of "heroes in medicine and music." Although he is a god, he suffers an incurable wound.[2] Chiron is a musical medicinal archetypal wounded healer who, because of this eternal wound, becomes a divine healer.

So why is Chiron, divine teacher of music, half horse and *not* half goat? Is there something special about the horse that can teach us something about music? I have spent a lot of time with horses and what I find most remarkable about them is their acute sense of smell and hearing. They also have an uncanny ability to perceive any subtle movements in their peripheral surroundings. Furthermore, they seem to possess the gift of clairvoyance and clairaudience in addition to being masters of perceiving our thoughts and feelings and thereby revealing ourselves to ourselves. Today horses are used in equine therapy for humans, showing themselves to be great healers of many psychological problems. Horses are wild, powerful creatures full of libido, life energy, which is what we need when we move in the world of song. There are also mythological stories about horses who can open wells with their hooves, and the winged horse Pegasus sprang from the head of Medusa, who could petrify anyone with her gaze. Pegasus opened a spring of creativity where the Muses later gathered and sang. The horse clearly can bring to us what we need when we sing, and if we can learn its way of attentive listening and suprasensory perception, our soul songs will take us closer to the Self. Just like the serpent, the horse is an invaluable guide on our musical individuation journey.

Some of the most moving words by von Franz are where she honours the instinctual and spontaneous wisdom of the horse. I believe what she writes below has to do with not only the way of Chiron or Orpheus and their musical intuitive communion with animals, but also with the challenging times we are living in today:

"The horse and its magical knowledge is more immediate and personal. It is a spontaneous reaction which springs from the deepest instinctual layer of the individual personality... because it is always improvised and springs in new form from the spontaneous basic nature of the psyche...

It is superior because it cannot be figured out by anybody else. As soon as you have codified knowledge of some kind, it can be misused. Evil forces can take possession of it and use it for their own purposes. But creative, instinctual spontaneity can never be foreseen, and the other can never tell what's going to happen. It is completely creative and essentially unforeseeable, and thus superior to other knowledge...

It is a kind of semi-unconscious reaction, it is the one thing which can overcome the attack of evil when that has taken form, when it has combined itself with a certain intelligence and with the tradition of the past… The real danger for us is when these forces combine with scientific intelligence, with the highest achievements of scientific knowledge… (but) in spite of everything, one thing superior to it: a return to the innermost genuineness of the depths of our own psyche with its invisible clairvoyance and natural knowledge. With this we can possibly overcome even these diabolical forces."[3]

Asclepios, who was trained in both medicine and music, is often, just like the musical Hermes, depicted with a serpent-entwined rod. The upward movement of the serpents symbolizes, according to Jungian analyst C.A. Meier "the process of becoming conscious."[4] The motif and image of the serpent around a staff can be compared to the story in the Old Testament about Moses in the desert where he held up a serpent and those who stared into its fiery eyes were healed. It is also said that Asclepios shapeshifted and became a serpent, which his patients experienced in their visions during the healing process.[5]

In the Asclepios myth, serpents and dogs have a curative role in the incubation time during which dreams could arrive and heal the wounds. In the temples of Epidaurus, they were often called upon to empathically lick the wounds of those who were suffering, as well as being the guardians of dreams – animal mediators between the world of gods and the world of humans.

Jacoby also emphasized that empathy in therapy has to do with emotions and strong instincts which could be deepened and integrated by learning about music since there are many resemblances between therapy and music. He said that "a psychoanalyst needs to reclaim the instinctual musician within since this will increase and deepen his or her empathic understanding of what is happening in the client." The whole musical and emotional experience with its moods, progression of chords, major or minor keys; the intervals, the distance between the notes and quality of the tones; the harmonies and dis-harmonies; the echo within and the echo from outside, is all part of the transformational harmonic experience. This can be felt when the temenos and psychic matrix between analyst and analysand emotionally resonates with a musical and instinctual empathy.[6]

As seen in the Greek myths, animals are very important in both music and medicine for empathic healing to take place. It is not just any animal that appears in the myths, however. Certain animals such as a serpent, a horse, and a dog, appear again and again which is why we can assume that there must be a deeper reason for this. I am sure that there are many more animals that are important, but I will focus on those mentioned above.

At the *Asclepeion*, the temple of Asclepios in Epidaurus, dogs were honored for their healing presence. Many goddesses are depicted together with dogs, such as the earth goddess Hecate who could even shapeshift into a dog. The musical god Apollo also had a strong connection to the wild relative of the dog, the wolf. Here we can also mention the dog Cerberus, the guardian of the underworld. In ancient Egypt we find Anubis, the psychopomp god of the underworld who was depicted with the head of a jackal. There are many myths and stories all over the world in which dogs have a divine role.

Jungian analysts Barbara Hanna and Eleanora Woloy have done extensive research into the archetypal symbolism of dogs. Hannah writes that in the Asclepian rituals at Epidaurus, the dogs cured different ailments by licking the ill and were considered as "the living vehicle for the power of the god." She also refers to Jung who considered saliva and spittle as "soul-substance," and therefore the licking could be seen as a way "the dog really massages us with the essence of its soul."[7]

Woloy, who uses her dog in her therapeutical work with clients, explores different motifs of how the archetype of the dog is expressed in mythology: "the helpful animal related to instinct; the dog as symbol of death and rebirth; the dog as psychopomp, or guide – in all instances the dog is the guide par excellence."[8] Woloy concludes: "Each time we stroke our dogs and in their affection they lick us, we can remember we are participating in one of the oldest healing rituals known to mankind."[9]

I have had many dogs in my life, and I am very grateful for their playful affection and instinctual teachings. As I mentioned earlier, most dogs are masters of deep listening, acute attention, and absolute presence – skills that are very important in the world of song and music, and in the world of therapy. We live in times where many young people seem to be losing these skills, and we have even coined diagnostic terms such as ADHD – Attention Deficit Hyperactivity Disorder. Could it be that from a deeper archetypal perspective the instinctual life is being lost? And then, is losing one's attention and listening skills only symptoms on the surface? And if so, no SSRI-pills will cure any real cause on a deeper level.

Diagnosis and medication are sometimes very important, but it must be done with ethical responsibility. During 2014 - 2016, I was involved in an extensive research project on the inflation of psychiatric diagnoses in our times and how Big Pharma gains huge profits from this. My research brought no uplifting stories, and this forced me to carefully reflect on what is going on in the depths and what is going on at the surface. I also had to ask questions about the state of our collective world, where humanity, at the speed of light, seems to be losing its instinctual animal sanity. As Dr. James Davies seriously asks: "Why are there more than 50 million antidepressant prescriptions in England alone each year? Why, without solid scientific justification, has the number of mental disorders risen from 106 in 1952 to around 370 today? In Britain alone, more than 20 per cent of the adult population take a psychiatric drug any one year: an increase of over 500 per cent since 1980. Despite this prescription epidemic, levels of mental illness of all types have increased."

The situation in the US is as tragic as in the UK and, since we are dealing with a global phenomenon, I am sure many other countries experience the same. Professor and chair of DSM-IV Task Force, Allen Frances, firmly protests against the medicalization of normality. He warns against the obsessive tendency to pathologize the slightest deviation from what the DSM bible has decided to be 'normal.' Frances also admits that the DSM Task Force did not manage to prevent Big Pharma from quickly taking advantage of the enormous increase of psychiatric diagnoses "reaping multi-billion dollar profits." Frances' book *Saving Normal – an*

Insiders Revolt Against Out-of-control Psychiatric Diagnosis, DSM-5, Big Pharma and the Medicalization of Ordinary Life is a sharp and authoritative critique of what is going on in some areas in the world of psychiatry and pharmaceutical industries.[10]

So, with all this diagnosing and pill-popping and even electro-shocking going on, I believe one must look at this collective 'disorder' with the instinctive eye of the soul. Psychiatry derives from the Greek word 'psyche' i.e., 'soul' but psychiatry unfortunately seems to have forgotten to include this word in the DSM. This means that the soul's dimension is not part of psychiatry's perspective on so called mental disorders. If a client comes into the praxis room and says he or she just had a wonderful conversation will a stranger – a street dog. Upon hearing this, do we directly reach for the DSM, or do we encourage the client's soul to tell the story of the divine dog?

According to Jung, every complex is connected to an archetype. What complex is Big Pharma then suffering from? Possibly a money-complex since it constantly is looking for more and more profit. To see through this money-complex we must search for its powerful archetype. What is money? Money is a magic transformer that can bring about miracles and disasters, and with Russell Lockhart's words, money is "a talisman," God-like.[11] We can therefore allow our souls to hypothesize that perhaps Big Pharma is suffering from a spiritual problem. Big Pharma obviously wants more and more money i.e., wants more and more talismanic power. Big Pharma might therefore unconsciously be longing for the power of God. There is a dark side to the archetype, and since time immemorial it has been known for its seducing power. Only our sane instincts can protect us from this seduction. Archaic man knew the importance of 'protective' incantations and it could be useful to reconnect to this archaic musical knowledge.

I like playing around with anagrams and cannot refrain from looking at the word 'dog' which when spelled backwards reads 'god.' If we are living in times when we are losing our instincts, losing our dog nature, might we also be losing our god nature? Both Jung and Neumann wrote that our lost gods have become our diseases. Could it then be that song and music could bring back our instinctual skills if we realign ourselves with the animals, with the gods? If so, music should, according to Jung, be an "essential part of every analysis" since it reaches the deep archetypal layers and strengthens our psyche's survival skills.

These reflections are, of course, partly hypothetical and could be considered a bit too instinctually wild. On the other hand, a soul tour into this wilderness could bring therapeutic musical wisdom and teachings. As some Greek philosophers have said, a bit of divine madness lifts the soul. Jungian analyst Albert Kreinheder wrote: "If you let yourself be crazy without losing your sanity, there is comfort and perhaps wisdom… (and) as Ann Landers says: A little craziness now and then could save you from permanent brain damage."[12]

When studying the way of dogs, it becomes apparent that they can help us in both therapy and in music as instinctual soul guides and playful teachers of attention, listening and presence. To bring them closer to the human world, instead of just treating them like pets or lower animals, it is good to be aware that dogs too have souls, and they do dream every night. There have been some interesting recent studies in neuroscientific and behavioral science which show the soulful life of animals. Professor David Pena-Guzmán has extensively researched the dream world of animals which shows that they are conscious beings. He demonstrates that they "run reality simulations while asleep, with a dream ego moving through a dynamic and coherent dreamscape." Guzmán writes that "animals who, even in the oceanic calmness of sleep, give birth to enigmatic and imaginary worlds from the deepest depths of their being."[13]

To awaken the soul, to be with animals as conscious beings, and live on this earth and treat her as an alive numinous luminous being, means to challenge the mechanistic and reductive dogmas of the spirit of our time. It demands of us to become aware of our instinctual dreams and to know that the Earth also dreams as do her living creatures. As Guzmán writes, quoting Professor Antonio Damasio in his book Descartes' Error: "our sense of who we are does not come, as Descartes believed, from above, from reason. It comes from below, from the slow and steady consolidation of emotionally coloured memories, including dream memories."[14]

The realization that animals are our equals challenges us to improve our ethical and moral obligations towards them and their world. To listen and learn from animals is one way of honoring them, and if we were to bring song and music into the analysis, as Jung proposed, we should perhaps not start with learning musical scales. That exercise comes later. Maybe the first initiation into the mystery of song is to reclaim the animal within and listen to its wise musical instinct, or as David Abram writes, perhaps go even deeper by "becoming animal."[15] Now and then, we need to take a deep breath and descend into the primordial realm, so that we can resonate and awaken the wild singing soul within us.

Orpheus – The Singing Shaman

"As to Orpheus, his myth displays several elements that can be compared to shamanic ideology and techniques. The most significant is, of course, his descent to Hades to bring back the soul of his wife Eurydice. At least one version of the myth has no mention of the final failure. The possibility of wresting someone from Hades is further confirmed by the legend of Alcestis. But Orpheus also displays other characteristics of a 'Great Shaman': his healing art, his love for music and animals, his 'charms', his power of divination. Even his character of 'culture hero' is not in contradiction to the best shamanic tradition. – Was not the 'first shaman', the messenger sent by God to defend humanity against diseases and to civilize it?"[16]

One aspect of the singer's journey can be called orphic. It is not a journey for all singers, but some of us seem to be drawn in this direction. Orpheus' presence tends to enter the temenos of song therapy. With the orphic aspect I mean that the myth of Orpheus is in action. Within this myth, with its many symbols and motifs, is the inspired singer, musician – the music archetype. Hypothetically, the mathematical archetype can also be in action since music, in an abstract way, is mathematics, rhythmical patterns and numbers in movement. These archetypes can be seen as facets of energetic configurations of the grand archetype of the Self.[17]

Orpheus was known for his divine musical gift. So soulfully moving was his lyre playing and sublime singing that even Hades, the lord of death and the underworld, opened his heart for a few seconds and gave Orpheus the chance to rescue his beloved Eurydice. In the official and best-known version of the myth, Orpheus fails in his mission and loses Eurydice. There are however other versions of the myth where his shamanic soul retrievals from the underworld are successful. Writer and musician Gary Lachman refers to the earlier original tales of Orpheus, as do Eliade and many other writers. Lachman notes: "In the earliest versions of the myth, Orpheus succeeds in freeing Eurydice from Hades; it was only in later versions that he fails, and the tale becomes a tragedy." It seems as though the myth is an enigma in a floating flux. Later the Roman writers – such as Ovid and Vergil, elaborated extensively on the tragic theme and re-composed the story of Orpheus.[18]

I often wonder why the cultural majority hold on to, and continuously stage, the version of the myth in which Orpheus fails? Those wonderings however belong to another book. My intuition tells me, though, that there could be both political and religious reasons for this, i.e., Orpheus' shamanic and healing approach to music could no longer fit into the cultural, institutional systems and religious dogmas of the new Attic times. His musical presence, mystical hymns and incantations could have been seen as a threat to the emerging power structures and therefore he had to be removed – written out of history. Against all odds however, and over thousands of years, Orpheus has kept returning to us, resurrecting himself and shapeshifting his being into countless musical dimensions. It needs a bit of soulful harmonic tuning to feel his invisible presence.

Professor of ethnomusicology Gianfranco Salvatore points out:

"Probably fuelled by religious polemics, the Attic civilization resisted the spreading influence of the figure of the magic citharode incarnated in Orpheus. Instead in its stories and even in its iconography the most malefic aspects of magical-religious practises

*were portrayed. Nevertheless, from the end of the XIV century B.C.
and in a wide area throughout the Eastern Mediterranean, Orpheus'
paradigm was present: a most beautiful symbol of the miraculous
powers that music has over living creatures, incarnated in the
mythological figure of a magic musician. A compelling, enchanting
power able to take away interest in any other activity and to engulf
animals in the magic experience of listening to music – a power that
song and lyre-playing exercised over the soul (a psychagogic
power…)*

*Within and outside the Greek culture, famous and popular, yet
ignored and feared by the religious establishment, and reflecting a
controversial intercultural heritage of ancient Mediterranean
imagery – Orpheus has symbolized, for 3500 years, both an
uncomfortable and magical reality: the idea that music has
immense power which might not necessarily be a divine gift but is
a formidable human resource and carrier of enchantment,
harmony and peace."*[19]

In a sense, the practice of shamanism can be subversive since the shamans show that through song and music we can be in deep contact with the spirits and the worlds of gods. No priest or other intermediary power person is needed. All it asks of us is to dare to go forth on our soul journey into the imaginal realm and to allow ourselves to be taken, to be seized and grasped by the hypnotic sound of a lyre, or the repetitive rhythms of a drum, or the trance of a rattle. The shamanic journey to the imaginal realm can of course also be made with a song or a chant as the divine transcendent musical vehicle.

The essence of the musical gift of Orpheus is deeply connected to soul and its capacity for crossing boundaries into other dimensions. Orpheus is as much in communion with the animals as he is with the gods – in balance with spirit and instinct. He navigates freely in both the upperworld and the underworld in which dimensions he retrieves souls back to the living. No other visitor to the underworld, except the psychopomp Hermes and the goddesses Hecate and Demeter, have managed to reach into the very heart of Hades and persuaded him to let go of what belongs to the land of the living. Persephone, the daughter of Demeter, was therefore allowed to ascend from the underworld half of the year instead of being confined there permanently.

Is there a connection between the Great Mother and Orpheus and does the serpent have anything to do with this connection? Jungian analyst Eric Neumann noted that the serpent is associated with the Great Mother archetype.[20] The earthbound animals definitively belong to her so one can assume that Orpheus was attuned to the vibrations, the rhythms and tones of the Great Mother as well as to the serpents who often dwell inside her dark caves. Orpheus was also, in his early years, aligned with Dionysus, the chthonic musical prophetic ecstatic god of the earth.

Orpheus had a magic ability to heal humans with his music. He could also spellbind, charm, and communicate with all animals and even enchant the gods. One often sees him depicted sitting with his lyre amid all kinds of furry four-legged and winged ones, often with a serpent close by. Jung pointed out how crucially important it is to include the animal realm in the religious iconical world. Orpheus included them, and in his spiritual and musical practice he was timely tuned into their mana.

> *"When the animals are no longer included in the religious symbol or creed, it is the beginning of the dissociation between religion and nature. Then there is no mana in it. As long as the animals are there, there is life in the symbol; otherwise, the beginning of the end is indicated."*[21]

Was Orpheus' deep connection to the animal world, and therefore to the instinctual, the reason why his music was said to have a healing power that could create miraculous cures? The myth tells us that Orpheus was given the lyre by Apollo who originally got it from Hermes. Hermes, just after he was born, made the lyre from a tortoise' shell and its strings from goat intestines which reveals that the lyre originates from the animal world.

Are animals closer to the gods, closer to the musical Self? Sometimes it seems as if they are, which is why animals can be inspiring soul teachers of the healing capacity of song and music.

Orpheus as Saviour

Another interesting fact about Orpheus is that his image merges with Christ's in the early Christian catacombs. Images of Orpheus playing the lyre appear in Christian burial art, and he sometimes appears as a shepherd, a symbolic identity he shares with Christ. They are both seen in the company of animals with the serpent close by.

Christ, just like Asclepios, the musical god of healing, can also shapeshift into a serpent and, as with Orpheus, is often portrayed as a friend of animals. In whichever way we interpret Christ's shapeshifting into the serpent depends on whether we associate the serpent as beneficial or malevolent, or perhaps both. There can be a strong connection between the Saviour and the 'musician' since their symbolism merge and, in addition to this, both have a deep connection to the serpent. King David, the ancestral father of Jesus, was also a master musician of the harp. The way he played the harp was so profoundly soothing, that it even calmed the dark melancholy of the old king Saul. We can therefore conclude that Christ is a descendant of an ancestral line where music was therapeutically and spiritually uplifting, and this fact deepens his relationship to Orpheus.[22]

There is also the Apollonian and the Dionysian side of music in Orpheus's life since he initially aligned himself with Dionysus, but in his last days turned to Apollo. These musical gods were perhaps not that different from each other as they both had a close connection to the serpent in one way or another – Apollo by taking over the serpent from the oracle, the Pythia of Delphi, and Dionysus who was in tune with the serpent by being a chthonic and oracular god of the earth. Then, of course, we also have the musical god Hermes with his divine serpent staff.

The Many Myths of Orpheus

One version of the myth tells us that Orpheus was killed by a group of raging Thracian women who were in a mad frenzy because he had turned his attention to Apollo and away from Dionysus. Perhaps they saw this as a betrayal. Did they also see it as a betrayal of the Great Mother? On some vases the mythical images also depict the Maenads tearing him apart. It is said that his head fell into the river Hebrus to be carried away by the currents. In other words, Orpheus was dismembered, just like the god Dionysus. We are also told that in time Orpheus' head floated up on the island of Lesbos where it was taken care of by the local people. They made him an altar where the oracular voice of Orpheus spoke until Apollo himself finally silenced it. The lyre of Orpheus was rescued by the Muses and placed among the stars in the heavens.

On the other hand, other versions of the myth of Orpheus tell us that he was *not* killed by the Thracian women or the Maenads. Instead, he is portrayed as a vibrant magical musician surrounded by Thracian women and men who seem to be deeply touched and soulfully moved by his music.[23]

All the myths about Orpheus seem to turn into a paradox. Most astounding is that what he is best known for in our Western culture, i.e., losing Eurydice to the underworld and later being killed, seems to never have happened at all! These stories seem to be completely made up by the spinning imaginations of our collective cultural elite! Many versions of the myth indicate that he never lost Eurydice to the underworld and that perhaps she never even existed at all. It also seems that he might not have been killed by the Thracian women or Maenads either. Being a mystic and a shaman, he might have been forced to withdraw and distance himself from the official political and collective religious scene. His spiritual path did not resonate with the rigid dogmas that ruled in his time.

For this reason, Orpheus probably took a step back into the periphery and became an outsider – an elusive leader of a spiritual group where music was used as medicine, for the healing of body, heart, and soul in devotional singing of prayers. What is said to be left of Orpheus' musical tradition are the Orphic Hymns – a series of incantations devoted to the gods. These hymns might have been composed by followers of his mystery cult whereas later followers might have recomposed the lyrics and composed new ones. The hymns were probably accompanied by lyres and drums and sung or recited like chants, rhythmically and resonantly, to this atmospheric musical accompaniment. One gets the impression that the chanted words were considered to contain a sublime hidden light which could attract the divine gaze of the gods.

The Orphic Hymns and Jung's Incantations

"The supreme god of Orphism was Dionysus and at the center of this religious faith was a cosmogony different from the one we learn from Hesiod's 'Theogony'. Orphism preached the simple idea that the world was born from an egg. This primordial egg hatched out the first god, Eros, who was later named Protogonos and Phanes and who was said to be both male and female. He then created the world."[24]

During a period of his life Jung was very "occupied with Orphism,"[25] and those who are familiar with his *Red Book* will recognize the god *Phanes* to whom Jung devoted deep attention through sublime paintings and lyrical incantations. The god *Phanes*, and the musical and devoted practice of incantations, seems to be a transcendent link between the life paths of Orpheus and of Jung. Both were treated as mystics and outsiders, at least if we look at how most of mainstream media and the high priests of psychological and religious dogmas have treated their teachings. I mean, how many versions of the Orpheus' myth are there, and how many varying tales about Jung? This book is not about Orpheus and Jung, but I find it worthwhile to mention these common denominators.

Jung rarely spoke or wrote about music, but that does not mean that he was indifferent to it. It is quite common that we keep silent about things that really matter, about those archetypal phenomena that we know are very powerful. The numen of the song and the mana of the gods might sometimes seal our lips. In his *Red Book* Jung writes:

"God's armor will make you invulnerable and invisible to the worst fools.

Take your God with you. Bear him down to your dark land…(and) secretly carry your God…
Hence do not wait until rawly bungling hands of men hack your God to pieces, but embrace him again, lovingly, until he has taken on the form of his first beginning.
Let no human eye see the much beloved, terribly splendid one… the nearness of God makes people rave. They tremble with fear and fury and suddenly attack one another in fratricidal struggles, since one senses the approaching God in the other.
So conceal the God that you have taken with you… Thus do not speak and do not show the God, but sit in a solitary place and sing incantations in the ancient manner."[26]

According to Jung singing "incantations in the ancient manner" is a way of being in deep musical resonance with God and sublime archetypal powers. To protect and to "conceal the God," our singing should be done "in a solitary place." This approach to singing, and to God, is an archaic shamanic way, the intention being to keep the sacred shielded from "fools" and collective power struggles. Neither music nor God, have anything to do with fashion or trends, nor the financial market, which is why we should not make a business out of what is holy. Music was originally used as a cure, to keep the tribe soulfully healthy and in holy communion with the gods.

One of the first Orphic hymns is dedicated to *Hekate*, the ancient earth goddess of the underworld, associated with the moon and an ally of all animals. Just like Hermes, she was known to appear at crossroads and to guard thresholds. She also had the shamanic ability to shapeshift into animal forms, and the gift to see through and beyond all mysterious veils. She is a liminal feminine chthonic guide to those souls who struggle their transitions in darkness. Already here, in the initial verses to Hekate, the blessings of the animals' instinctive energy are chanted in a devoted way:

"I call the beloved goddess of the roads
and places where three ways meet. Heavenly,
earthly, and in the sea…

lover of solitude, who delights in deer,
the nocturnal goddess, protector of dogs…
and key-bearer to all the universe…
I pray you, maiden, to attend these rites…"[27]

In connection to the hymn of Hekate comes the mysterious chant to *Night*, mother goddess of darkness and the daughter of Phanes. It is a profound hymn which gives us the insight that darkness is as numinous and as important as light. Many of the hymns also give instructions about which specific incense should be used to the different chants, as though the fragrance of the incense could enhance the power of the incantation. The text states that the incense of firebrands should be used with the hymn to Night, as though fire is needed in the darkness to transform the chanting way into the goddess of Night. We can also read that Night is in the company of horses. Once again, the animal archetype is united with the numinous energies.

"I will sing of Night, the mother of gods
and of humans. Nyx, the source of all things…
hear me, blessed goddess shining in the dark sky,
filled with bright stars, rejoicing in silent
nights of sleeping peace… mother of dreams…
giver of sleep, friend to all, night shining,
you lead your horses forth…
You send forth light into the depths…
kindly come, and drive back the fears of night"[28]

The sixth Orphic hymn is devoted to the god *Protogonos* (firstborn, primeval). Athanassakis writes that he is "one of the most important figures in Orphic cosmological speculation. This being has many appelations: *Phanes* (Bright One), *Metis* (Counsel, Resourcefulness, Wisdom), *Eubouleus* (He of Good Counsel), *Antau*ges (The One Reflecting Light), *Eros,* among others. He shares with *Dionysos* the names *Eubouleus, Erikepaios,* and *Bromos,* and is indeed even identified at times with Dionysos himself."[29] Phanes is an androgynous god, born from an egg and appears as a creator-god with golden wings and shapeshifting animal faces (serpent, ram, bull, lion). He caused both the universe and the gods to emerge, and he gave birth to his daughter goddess Night. Since he is in communion with Dionysos there is chtonic primordial music in his divine being.

Just like the Orphic Hymns, Jung opens his *Red Book* incantations with an enchanting invocation that seems to be directed to Phanes. He is also alluding to the old Greek practice of 'incubation' which can open communion with the gods where healing can take place.[30]

> *"Set the Egg before you, the God in his beginning.*
> *And behold it.*
> *And incubate it with the magical warmth of your gaze."*

The Orphic hymn to *Protogonis – Phanes*, advises us to use the incense of Myrrh when reciting the many names of this god. In this invocation he is also honoured as a bringer of light:

> *"I call Protogonos, two-natured, great*
> *wind-striding, egg-born, fluttering golden*
> *wings in delight, bull-roaring. Begetter*
> *of blessed ones and of mortal humans:*
> *much remembered…*
> *ineffable hidden whirling bright scion…*
> *to the universe you brought bright and holy*
> *light, and so I call you Phanes…*
> *come with joy to the initiators*
> *of this most intricate and holy rite…"*[31]

Athanassakis writes that in the transcendent rituals of the Orphic Hymns:

> *"The magic of song, devotional, undulant, filled all the sacred space*
> *and provoked the human heart to seek union with the divine…*
> *Clearly, elevation of mood and the powerful affirmation of a*
> *meaningful and bonding presence are elements that run through*
> *the recitation of mighty words and sacred sounds flowing into the*

eager ears and souls of the faithful. Even the puns serve this purpose. Names chanted or yet better sung or simply recited in a particular sacred tone have power. Each epithet reverberates into the mind of the celebrant and spins out its own plot and its own action. As one epithet follows another, chains of meaning and sound acquire power that may exceed that of a highly structured narrative."[32]

The law of attraction states that 'like attracts like,' and Jung seems to have been attracted to the shamanic musician Orpheus. Orpheus knew the secret of the incantations – the hymns and songs, whose melodic and rhythmic words became magnets that drew him closer to the gods. Perhaps also Jung sensed that the very center of our Being, the Self, is sublime music, and that the musical devotion of our souls draws us deep into the unfathomable divine musical resonance of the *mysterion*.

Jungian analyst Josephine Evetts-Secker writes about the language of the soul and the archetypal forces that are in motion when we speak and write. She means that: "in our work as analysts and in our living experience of psyche, we need to return to the poets to refresh 'the thoughts of our hearts'. We need to restore the poet within to revitalize the speech of our souls and the language of our psychologies."[33]

In the "Incantations" in the *Red Book* it seems as though Jung is seriously trying to write from the depth of his heart, and he reclaims the poet within while reciting the words rhythmically, in the form of a prayer, when he calls upon the ultimate source.

> *"Amen, you are the lord of the beginning.*
> *Amen, you are the lord of the East.*
> *Amen, you are the flower that blooms over everything.*
> *Amen, you are the deer that breaks out of the forest.*
> *Amen, you are the song that sounds far over the water.*
> *Amen, you are the beginning and the end…*
>
> *Rise up you gracious fire of old night.*
> *I kiss the threshold of your beginning."*[34]

ENDNOTES

[1] Walter F. Otto, *The Muses and the Divine Origin of Singing and Speech*, quoted from Karl Kerényi, *Asclepios – Archetypal Image of the Physician's Existence*, (transl. Ralph Mannheim), Thames and Hudson (Bollingen Foundation), 1959, p. xxiv.

[2] Karl Kerényi, *Asclepios – Archetypal Image of the Physician's Existence*, (transl. Ralph Mannheim), Thames and Hudson (Bollingen Foundation), 1959, p. 97.

[3] Marie-Louise von Franz, *Shadow and Evil in Fairytales*, Shambhala Publications, 1995, pp. 293 - 294.

[4] C.A. Meier, *Healing Dream and Ritual – Ancient Incubation and Modern Psychotherapy*, Daimon Verlag, 1989, p. 68.

[5] Ibid.

[6] Supervision sessions in Jungian song therapy with Dr. Mario Jacoby 2010/ 2011.

[7] Barbara Hannah, *The Archetypal Symbolism of Animals*, p. 86 – 87.

[8] Eleanora M. Woloy, *The Symbol of the Dog in the Human Psyche*, Chiron Publications, 1990, p. 4.

[9] Ibid., p. 72.

[10] Allen Frances, *Saving Normal – An Insider's Revolt Against out-of-control Psychiatric Diagnosis, DSM - 5, Big Pharma and the Medicalization of Ordinary Life*, William Morrow/ HarperCollins Publishers, 2013.
James Davies, *Cracked – Why Psychiatry is Doing More Harm than Good*, Icon Books, 2014, back cover.
James Davies, *Sedated – How Modern Capitalism Created Our Mental Health Crisis*, Atlantic Books, 2022, back cover.

[11] Russell A. Lockhart, *Silver, Change, Imagination*, (in conversation with Rob Henderson, www.ralockhart.com).

[12] Albert Kreinheder, *Body and Soul - the Other Side of Illness*, Inner City Books, 2009, p. 19.

[13] David M. Pena-Guzmán, *When Animals Dream – the Hidden World of Animal Consciousness*, Princeton University Press, 2022, p. 192.

[14] Ibid., p. 188.

[15] David Abram, *Becoming Animal – an Earthly Cosmology*, Pantheon Books, 2010.

[16] Mircea Eliade, *Shamanism – Archaic Techniques of Ecstasy*, Bollingen Foundation, Princeton University Press, 1992 (origin. 1964), p. 391.
For more explorations into shamanism see Michael Harner, *The Way of the Shaman*, Sandra Ingerman, *Soul Retrieval* and *Awakening to the Spirit World*, (co-ed. Hank Wesselman), and Jeanne Achterberg, *Imagery in Healing – Shamanism and Modern Medicine*.

[17] Marie-Louise von Franz, *Number and Time – Reflections Leading toward the Unification of Depth Psychology and Physics*, 1974.

[18] Gary Lachman, *Lost Knowledge of the Imagination*, Floris Books, 2020, p. 25 and 142. *The Mysteries – Papers from the Eranos Yearbooks*, ed. Joseph Campbell, Bollingen Series XXX Vol.2. Princeton University Press, 1990, p. 68. (Walter Wili "The Orphic Mysteries and the Greek Spirit").
W.K.C. Guthrie, *Orpheus and Greek Religion*, Princeton University Press, original print 1952, paperback print 1993, p. 31, Ann Wroe, *Orpheus – the Song of Life*, Pimlico, 2012, Algis Uzdavinys, *Orpheus and the Roots of Platonism*, The Matheson Trust, 2011, p. 41, Gianfranco Salvatore, *Orpheus before Orpheus*, Spring 71 – *Orpheus*, A Journal of Archetype and Culture, ed. Nancy Cater, Spring Journal 2004, pp. 171 - 191.

[19] Gianfranco Salvatore, *Orpheus before Orpheus*, Spring 71 – *Orpheus*, A Journal of Archetype and Culture, ed. Nancy Cater, Spring Journal 2004, pp. 184 - 186.

[20] Eric Neumann, *The Great Mother – an Analysis of an Archetype*, Princeton University Press, 1972 and *Art and the Creative Unconscious*, Princeton University Press, 1974.

[21] Carl Gustav Jung, *Visions*, Spring Publications, 1976, p. 284.

[22] *The Holy Bible* and www.biblegateway.com, Samuel 16:14-23.

[23] Gianfranco Salvatore, *Orpheus before Orpheus*, Spring 71 – *Orpheus*, A Journal of Archetype and Culture, ed. Nancy Cater, Spring Journal 2004, pp. 176 - 177.

[24] Apostolos N. Athanassakis and Benjamin M. Wolkow, *The Orphic Hymns*, John Hopkins University Press, 2013, p. xiv.

[25] Carl Gustav Jung, *The Structure and Dynamics of the Psyche*, Collected Works Vol. 8, p. 444.

[26] Carl Gustav Jung, *The Red Book – Liber Novus*, A Readers Edition, ed. Sonu Shamdasani, transl. Mark Kyburz, John Peck and Sonu Shamdasani, Philemon Series, The Foundation of the Works of C.G. Jung, W.W. Norton & Company, 2009, pp. 297 - 298.

[27] Patrick Dunn, *The Orphic Hymns*, Llewellyn Publications, 2022, p. 41.

[28] Ibid., p. 45.

[29] Ibid., p. 81.

[30] On 'incubation' in ancient Greece, see C.A. Meier, *Healing Dream and Ritual – Ancient Incubation and Modern Psychotherapy*, and Peter Kingsley, *In the Dark Places of Wisdom*.

[31] Patrick Dunn, *The Orphic Hymns*, p. 51.

[32] Apostolos N. Athanassakis, *The Orphic Hymns*, p. xvii and p. xxi.

[33] Josephine Evetts-Secker, *At Home in the Language of the Soul – Exploring Jungian Discourse and Psyche´s Grammar of Transformation*, Spring Journal Books, 2012, p. 5.

[34] Carl Gustav Jung, *The Red Book – Liber Novus*, A Reader's Edition, pp. 300 - 301.

CHAPTER VII
Song Therapy and Creativity

"The voice, our original and primary instrument for expression and communication, is the only instrument in which the player and played upon are contained within the same organic form."[1]

The human voice is deeply connected to our inner world and in its tones and timbres we can hear the soul and the psyche in motion. As Paul Newham, pioneering founder of Voice Movement Therapy and author of 'The Singing Cure', said during my VMT-training: "We can experience and perceive the voice as an embodied symbol for life itself."[2] The songs we sing can function as healing containers since they have a musical structure which can hold the strong emotions that surface when we sing. If the voice is grounded in the body, and the song is connected to soul and psyche, then the act of singing becomes a potential therapeutic vessel. "Art orders emotion at the deepest levels of consciousness, and it has a scope that can contain the most complex feelings."[3] In song we can also be in profound communion with the Self.

Jung often mentioned that the spiritual need of man is a human instinct and should be channeled through creative means that are suited for each individual. From my experience, there also seems to be a deep human musical need – an inherent archetypal instinct to sing. To prevent sickness of soul, or even loss of soul, this 'singing instinct' must be soulfully nourished. The musicologist Victor Zuckerkandl emphasized that:

"Man is a musical animal, that is, being predisposed to music and in need of music, a being that for its full realization must express

itself in tones and owes it to itself and to the world to produce music. In this sense, musicality is not something one may or may not have, but something that – along with other factors – is constitutive of man... Music is the concern of all, not of a privileged elite, and if musicality represents an asset, it is not the prerogative of a chosen few, but an endowment of man as man."[4]

Music teachers are generally not trained in psychology and neither do most musical institutions require of them to do any in-depth soul searching before they start their teaching careers. This can have serious effects on the psyches and souls of their students. In ordinary schools there are sadly not enough hours of music studies on the weekly schedule. This is a paradox since science has long since proven that studying and practicing music increases other skills simultaneously, like language and mathematics.

A good music teacher enhances our musical skills and lifts our psyches to brilliant heights, whereas a bad music teacher can push us into dark abysses. With 'bad,' I mean a music teacher who lacks empathy and projects his or her own musical frustrations and inner critics onto the students. I have encountered these students in my song-therapy courses, and some have very deep wounds from having been harshly corrected and shamed in front of others while trying to sing. This may cause them to internalize a judgemental authority voice which confuses their psyches and one can then hear them saying the standard defensive statement: "I cannot sing, I never could and I never will." This could be called a 'singing complex.'[5]

This firm and negative decision by these wounded people serves partly as a protective shield so that they do not have to re-experience the fear and trauma that the soul felt when judged so harshly in song (in musical communion with the Self). This defensive attitude in all its versions needs therefore to be respected as an "archetypal defense"[6] adopted by the soul. On the other hand, if there is ego stability one can slowly and carefully start to unveil and track the origin of the singing complex. One usually finds its roots in un-pedagogical music lessons in school. The family circle can also breed this singing shadow complex where unconscious parents project their own negative complexes on their children or even favour one child as the singer and expel the other as tone-deaf.

Based on many years of experience, I believe that there are no tone-deaf people unless the inner labyrinth of the ear has been surgically removed. There are instead a lot of soul-deaf people on this earth and this soul-deafness is usually accompanied by huge power complexes. If these power ridden people get to freely exercise their authority in whichever superior role they can grab hold of, it is a great threat to the soul of those who can still listen. This is extremely detrimental to the sensitive singer within (the singing soul-child).

Most of us have an inherent instinctual knowledge of the elementary basics of music. We respond and resonate in a natural way to music and even though we do not have the exact words for what is happening within us, we feel the reverberations in our depths. Victor Zuckerkandl strongly asserts:

"The experience of great music does not presuppose a special gift or learning. This is precisely the unique thing about music: it speaks a language that is understood without learning, understood by everyone, not just by the so-called musical people… in some instinctive way we understand the tonal language – that is, all of us, not just those that have learned it from a teacher."[7]

In the earlier chapters of this book, I emphasized the importance of reclaiming our instinctual side – the singing instinct – so that by singing we can heal our body and soul. I have also shown how singing can be a way to resonate in deep communion with the gods and the numinous energies in the imaginal realm.

To liberate the singing voice is a step-by-step journey and before any musical move, we must first become conscious of the way we breathe and the depth of our feelings and get in touch with the ground on which we stand. This can sound like a simple thing to do, but in practice, the simplest things in life are often what we find hardest to do. Our incapacity to keep things simple is why I have suggested that we try to learn from the animal world since most animals breathe and feel naturally. Many also fly with superior finesse while others walk steadily on their holy ground.

Our breath is connected to our emotions. When we feel fear our breathing gets shallow and when we feel relaxed our breathing deepens. People who have repressed emotions will often resist opening the breath since a deeper breathing will bring up any repressed emotion. Therefore, some people need to feel safe and held in the presence of a therapist before this emotional release can happen. As I wrote earlier, breath is also connected with spirit, so when we start breathing more deeply, we come closer to the spiritual realm. To breathe deeply with an open mouth (as singers must do) can also cause a feeling of having landed in the wilderness. We are in the unknown Other land and we are finally free. However, freedom is not something all of us have experienced or been allowed, and therefore we do not know what we are missing. Sadly, some of us are more comfortable behind bars. Singing, and life, are not about being comfortable though. It is about so much more.

To feel our feelings truly, and honestly, does not come naturally for some of us. What I mean by this, is that we must *honestly* and *truly* feel our feelings, and not just *imagine* or *pretend* that we are feeling something that we are not feeling. Allowing ourselves to truly feel takes time and practice. To become aware of and accept what we truly feel requires self-love and soul-compassion. Learning to trust and act on what we truly feel can take a lifetime. Therefore, we must daily ask ourselves: how do I truly and honestly feel and then embrace the inner response from the heart. Singing is about feeling and sounding simultaneously, truly feeling and truly sounding from the heart.

Now to our feet! Where are they? The Spanish poet Lorca said that the "duende" power of deep flamenco song rises from the earth up through one's feet, ascending upwards inside one's whole body. Can we feel our feet touching the earth? Some of us are not fully present in our bodies. Some of us live our lives in our heads since this is what has been rewarded by parental figures and teachers. What has been prioritized in our culture is to deliver facts from the head, i.e. the intellect. To ask people, who have mostly relied on their intellect, to descend all the way down to their feet can bring up in them a strong feeling of losing power and safety. To get them to truly feel their feet standing steadily on the ground can therefore take time. This is however a crucial descent since the singing soul – the vibrating life essence – needs the whole body. That is the way of the song of the soul.

By deepening the breath, by feeling what we truly feel, makes us aware that the act of singing is a very naked and vulnerable act. It is also a very powerful and animating act. The emotional reactions we get when we liberate the singing body and soul can therefore be strong and we become conscious of all repressive voices we have internalized. The expressive act of liberating the voice brings up tears, fears, and anger as well as ecstasy and joy. What we resist persists. The realization and integration of the paradox of strength in vulnerability is important for those who want to sing with emotional presence. It takes time, and there will be no healing through song unless we are willing to revisit our wounded hearts. It is only then that this psychic transformation and integration can happen.

The song-therapeutic process reconnects the heart and the soul to the song since singing touches both heart and soul directly. Music therapist Diane Austin presents vocal psychotherapy in "three com-plementary ways: as a creative experience in the here and now, as a bridge to the unconscious so that repressed and dissociated psychic contents can come to consciousness through playing with sounds and words, and as a symbolic language."[8]

While singing our souls back home[9], there is also an additional dimension to having tasted the serpent's forbidden fruit. This can be a numinous experience since soul tuning brings us into musical communion with the Self. The experience of the musical power of the Self is what many clients share as a deeply healing moment while singing. As a therapist, it is a feeling of grace to be present at those moments when soul re-connects with song and Self – a realization that usually comes to the client after a long period of psychospiritual preparation. It needs a long and deep musical incubation in the divine heart.

Today's science is very focused on how song and music affect the brain. I would wish that more scientists would turn their attention to the heart and see what is being moved by song inside this sacred chamber. However, there are some scientists doing research on the heart as an intelligent and perceptive organ which is welcome compensatory research.[10] Or perhaps it would be better to just leave the heart alone. Referring to Corbin, the subtle Heart knows the divine mystery of sound and love, and this profound knowing needs no scientific proof. It needs a song.

Stephen Harrod Buhner illuminates us on the heart:

"The human heart generates an electromagnetic field that can be measured up to 10 feet from the body's surface, though it extends much further than that. The field is 5000 times stronger than that generated by the brain. You can, in fact, feel the heart field of another person if you simply walk slowly up to them…
The crucial thing is to establish a synchronization between the heart field of the person and the therapist. The client will then begin using the heart field of the therapist as a model for integrative behaviour."[11]

So, in resonance with the heart, while vocalizing and voicing sounds, we might also feel as though we are taking part in a subversive psychic and chthonic underground (serpentine) act. I would even call it an individuation act of deeper dimensions, since reclaiming one's true voice and singing capacity is a way to reclaim one's true identity and wholeness – all that one is meant to be.

I do not mean that anyone can become a professional singer overnight – it takes long practice to master this musical craft. With some clients it can take many sessions to slowly return from the lofty heights of the logos down to Mother Earth and back into the body – the seat and home of the soul. Life has taught me that there is a potential singer within each and every one of us and we must make sure the singing seed does not fall on barren soil. Jung tells us that in many sagas and tales "the hero has snake eyes."[12] In song therapy one can actually see a different gleam in the eyes of those beginners who have just brought home their singing soul. It is that kind of shining trickster serpent gaze that says, "no longer will I be hindered by repressive voices, nor be hindered by the talents of others. Now I know how to sing and that is what I will do."

Another psychospiritual aspect of singing (and composing songs) is our relationship to our own creativity. Here I mean creativity in general, all the arts of the Muses: literature, poetry, painting, theatre, photography, dancing and much more. Practicing one form of the arts can release another creative art form. Jung wrote about how liberating it was for him to reconnect to his inner playful child and how this is the golden key to all creativity. A playful child usually moves from one creative act to another – a bit of painting here, a bit of singing there, lining up the dolls in order, bringing the toy animals into the stable, putting all the crayons back in their favourite box, and then … back to painting and singing again.

As Jung's *Red Book* shows, he found painting very illuminating for other dimensions in his life. He also enjoyed playing with stones and pieces of wood in the river. He wrote that these creative acts animated and liberated his own analytical writings on depth psychology – the *Collected Works*. He said: "Often the hands know how to solve a riddle with which the intellect has wrestled in vain."[13] He wrote:

"First I made the observations, and only then did I hammer out my views. And so it is with the hand that guides the crayon or brush, the foot that guides the dance-step, with the eye and the ear, with the word and the thought: a dark impulse is the ultimate arbiter of the pattern, an unconscious 'a priori' precipitates itself into plastic form… Over the whole procedure there seems to reign a dim foreknowledge not only of the pattern but of its meaning. Image and meaning are identical; and as the first takes shape, so the latter becomes clear. Actually, the pattern needs no interpretation: it portrays its own meaning."[14]

From my own experience as a professional artist, we can turn to painting and/or dancing to liberate our singing voice. I have found these mercurial movements back and forth between expressive artistic realms very freeing and inspiring. I often paint when I feel stuck in my singing, and I turn to singing when I do not find the right image in my work with photography. These movements free our libido from the temporary psychic impasse, and these creative voyages liberate psychic energy that sometimes moves the artist into the timeless, visionary, and clairvoyant space where future events can be predicted.

Singing is not just nonverbal music; it is also about the word. In the Bible it is written that "In the beginning was the Word and the Word was with God, and the Word was God." It is also written: "And God said "Let there be Light: and there was Light."[15] This indicates that the sounded word is holy and profoundly creative and Jungian analyst Russell A. Lockhart writes that "the powerful image of God creating by and through the word… (it) is God speaking the world and its creatures into being… the word is seed and gives birth to life and living things."[16]

This means that when we are sounding words, we are potentially setting powerful energies in motion. The more truth and soul we add to the word the more numinous becomes its power – the word of God. Some people have an issue with the concept of God, and some have an issue with power, while some have an issue with both. This can give rise to tension in individuals who have been shamed and tamed to behave in restricted ways and seduced to believe in a mechanistic and reductive world view. Liberated speaking, sounding, and singing is to reclaim power and be a channel for archetypal energies. It is not an egoistic act; it is an act of service to something higher and deeper.

There are some people who fear their own creativity, sometimes without even knowing it. Becoming conscious of and reclaiming and expressing one's own creativity can feel challenging since it entails transforming the old and creating the new. One part of the trans-formational act is destruction, i.e., dissolving what was once valid, but no longer serves or nourishes soul. Another difficult part is leaving behind the old, all that is now passé, and to courageously move into the new domain of the soul. Jungian analyst and film director Juliet Miller has worked with many female singers who do not struggle with stage fright, but are quite comfortable singing on stage. Instead, they struggle with their fear of truly coming home to themselves and thereby owning their creativity and their power to transform.

> *"By using art that expresses itself through constant movement, singers have in their power a force for change, which may move and affect both themselves and an audience. It can be frightening to be in possession of such a power, and as a result singers frequently try to exert control over and to limit their voices. They may feel that, by singing, they are playing with fire in having the ability to arouse and stir up both themselves and an audience. As a result, they can sometimes express feelings of either being burnt or of the fear of being burnt by the profession they have chosen."*[17]

To sound the voice is to come into being. To give name is to become distinct and to enter the world and words of human beings. To name gives a sense of knowing. To sound the knowing is to emerge and become visible and audible to the world. To sing the knowing is to increase and further one's worldly presence. Some of us fear our own knowing and presence in the world as we may have a history of having been judged by parental and authoritative figures. Because of this, we do our best to hide our wounded souls behind an indistinct and timid voice and a submissive and obedient persona. We are not to be blamed; in therapy we are to be listened to since this is about our soul wound. When the soul is wounded, we are dealing with serious matters. To quote Jungian analyst Diane Cousineau Brutsche who writes about *Lady Soul*: "soul means one's own deepest identity, the very core of one's psyche… she is the active subject of the transcendent function, while being, like the alchemical stone, at the same time its means and its goal."[18] To heal the soul can therefore also mean to heal the transcendent function – the numinous mediator between the human and the spiritual realms.

Some songs can heal, as can some words. The Sufi musician Hazrat Inayat Khan spent his whole life studying and teaching the mysticism of music, sound, and word. He considered music superior to all the other arts, a healing agent leading the soul back to the divine God. Khan was a professional musician of the Indian string instrument, the Vina. For Khan, playing music was a spiritual practice where one could come into harmony with the Divine. He writes that the whole basis of creation is movement, and that the "finest aspect of movement is what is called vibration." Music is vibration and so are sounded words. However, not all songs, and not all words, resonate in depth. Some songs just linger on the surface, and some sounded words and sentences just hang in mid-air without real substance. To quote Khan:

> *"The power and effect of any particular word depends upon the state in which that person was. It depends from what depth the word rises, and upon that depends the power and light of that word… The word will have power according to the illumination of the soul… in accordance with the divine spirit which is in the word, that word has life, power and inspiration."*[19]

When I ask myself what I have been doing all these years as a song therapist my answer is that I have been working with song as a therapeutic container and transformative alchemical vessel. I have tried to be of service to the musical Self by singing. Journeying between the personal realm and the transpersonal dimension, I have tried to help my clients to liberate their voices and embody the song. This strengthens their connection to their true feelings and to their instinctive singing soul within them. The intention is to sing with true presence and soulful vitality and to mend the broken singing wings so that the soul can ascend to the divine heights that only the soul knows the limits of.

I never felt alone when doing my song therapeutic work. I always felt as though I had a mysterious presence beside me, as if I was a servant of song, guided by an unspeakable and unfathomable musical energy. One could describe this experience as though Hermes and Orpheus had moved into the metaphysical dimension of my singing. They called on my attention as subtle teachers from the imaginal realm. They held that darkness and that light that neither I nor my clients could hold alone. In joy and in sorrow, Hermes and Orpheus have been my mercurial guides to musical animal wisdom, angelic transcendence, and subliminal perception. It has been an invaluable ineffable experience for which I am truly grateful. It has been an experience of the wild singing soul, and as Jungian analyst Clarissa Pinkola Estés notes: "If we will sing the song, we can call up the psychic remains of the wild soul and sing her into a vital shape again… To sing means to use the soul-voice."[20]

Let The Song In

How then can we integrate more music and song into our lives and into the world of therapy, and how do we "harness the profound merit of auditory symbols?"[21] I believe it is not as difficult as it may sound. As I have tried to demonstrate in this book, singing is not only about musical practices, though they are important. The voice is the inner instrument that is profoundly connected to our soul and heart. If the singing voice has been harshly judged, so too has the soul and the heart. Here then is where our journey must begin – in the soul and in the heart. The soul is both powerful *and* vulnerable, and the heart a very sensitive and perceptive organ. As I wrote earlier, the heart also remembers and as the French author Blaise Pascal said: "The heart has its reasons that reason does not know."[22]

One way to introduce songs into the therapeutic room is by asking the client to bring along songs that they are emotionally moved by. This can be especially useful for those clients who cannot remember their dreams. A song is like a dream and can potentially have the same evocative power. Singing can become an active imagination, like dreaming with open eyes. A song usually has a story and a series of symbols and images, and an abundance of feelings too, of course. Most of us long to thaw our frozen hearts and this is where song can become a pathway to the heart. Here it is important to not interpret or intellectually over-analyse the song.

It is better to let our feelings guide us and to let our inner singing child spontaneously find the labyrinthine way into the song.

In singing there is nothing that needs to be understood in minute detail, only enhanced, felt, and sounded. To just let our souls resonate with the song can be very healing. Songs can be like dreams in motion, transpersonal poetical experiences in musical time. They can have a deep effect on our psyche without being cognitively understood, as can dreams. To quote Jung:

> "But if dreams produce such essential compensations, why are they not understandable? I have often been asked this question. The answer must be that the dream is a natural occurrence, and nature shows no inclination to offer her fruits gratis or according to human expectations. It is often objected that the compensation must be ineffective unless the dream is understood. This is not so certain, however, for many things can be effective without being understood."[23]

Songs bring back memories, they are messengers from Mnemosyne, the goddess of memory. Songs and music are guarded by the Muses, the daughters of Mnemosyne. The word music comes from the ancient Greek word "mousike," which means the art of the Muses. Music exists in time, lives in time, but it can also transport us back and forth in time and magically move us outside of chronological time, into what the Greeks called "Kairos." These musical movements in time through song are often experienced as numinous and mystical.

So, just by acquainting ourselves with this aspect of song – as containers of memories – we are opening us to their healing power. Certain songs can remind us of situations in our past. Their evocative power brings us there, moves us back into memories to once again experience the feelings connected to that memory. In a safe therapeutic space, we can then express the feelings we might have repressed in the past. Here is where song can have a profound cathartic effect. We can talk about the song, but the cathartic release can be even more profound if both the client and the therapist sing the song together. Initially it is better to not sing the whole song, but to just sing a verse, a chorus line, or a few sentences. It is *not* a singing lesson, it is song therapy, and therefore all critical voices should be kept at bay – firmly blocked out from the temenos. If your inner critics persist and still manage to slip in, well then, just bring them out into the bright light so they can be clearly seen and heard, and then take these little critics by their necks and ask them *whom they serve* and then send them back to whom they belong.

For clients who are not skilled singers it is better to start with simple songs. Lullabies, for example, can be very soothing and, of course, bring back memories of early childhood. It is not up to the therapist to decide what songs should be brought to the session; the choice of songs must be left to the client. I do not believe that certain music and songs are more 'healing' than others. The specific kind of music that heals us is a very personal choice and these musical decisions must be respected. Of course, music that is too noisy and loud and hurts our ears is not to be recommended. I believe we need different songs in the various phases of our lives. We can apply Jung's concept of *individuation* when we remember how certain songs moved us. We can thread these songs like pearls on a musical string and resonate with them – the songs of individuation – the songs from each stage of our lives. First, we perhaps had the gentle lullabies that made us feel safe and sent us smoothly into dreamland. Then there might have been the sweet pop songs about love that opened our teenage hearts to the power of Eros. After that we perhaps discovered the powerful hard rock ballads that could send us to heaven or hell. Then along came the solitary folk singers who might have mirrored our spiritual longing with poetic words that resonated in the chambers of our heart. We also have, of course, the worlds of classical music with their grand operas and symphonies that might have swept us into visions of tragedy or joy. For some of us who travelled the world our ears were opened to exotic rhythms and meandering tunes that seemed foreign and yet familiar. Looking back at our musical soul journey, holding and living with this string of song memories is a way to nourish and heal our souls.

There are many underlying, emotional reasons to why we are attracted to certain songs. We may think we know all the reasons, but the more we sing the song, the more it reveals itself and our selves – if we pay attention. We must allow what moves us and then open to the feelings that surface, to follow what William Blake called the "golden strings." To quote Jungian analyst and musician Patricia Skar: "we realize that the music we are drawn to often contains dynamic qualities that connect to undiscovered sides of ourselves. Working on this music brings into consciousness not only rejected parts of our personalities, but also sides of ourselves that have never been in consciousness."[24]

When we learn to sing it is best to not set our ambitions too high. We must be careful not to beat ourselves up by choosing a song that we are not technically ready for. On the other hand, consistently picking difficult songs which block our first attempts at basic singing could also be a therapeutic subject to investigate. There is such a thing as the 'masochistic complex,' and this shadow takes great pleasure in self-torture, while crushing the inner artist and ruining the singing of the song. In song therapy it is important to keep the inner child safe and make sure that there is a dimension of childlike play in the therapeutical space. Many of us have been criticized when trying to sing. Here the therapist's role has a reparative role, a non-judgmental and positive mirror which the client can integrate neuron by neuron, song by song.

To enter the transpersonal realm, we must first deal with the personal realm, otherwise it could be comparable to spiritual bypassing. The unhealed wounds in our personal history hide the gates to the transpersonal realm and to the gods. When we let the songs lead us, we unveil and touch the wound. Transformation takes place when we are profoundly present and express the pain the wound has caused us. This can bring us closer to the gods. Quoting Jung:

"It is of course impossible to free oneself from one's childhood without devoting a great deal of work to it… Nor can it be achieved through intellectual knowledge only; what is alone effective is a remembering that is also a re-experiencing…

This 'personal unconscious' must always be dealt with first, that is made conscious, otherwise the gateway to the collective unconscious cannot be opened."[25]

For therapists who are inexperienced singers, it can be worth giving singing a try again. Singing songs inside the temenos will animate the therapeutic process. It will probably also heal the therapist's own singing complex which will then benefit both her/him and the clients. There are psychologically mature singing teachers out there, as well as voice and music therapists that we can learn from. We can also teach ourselves to sing. Initially we can copy other singers that we are inspired by, like children do when they learn something new. Then comes repetition which can be seen as a sacred ritual, and not something boring and tedious. This is how we enter the song – word by word, sentence by sentence, verse by verse, until the heart remembers the tonal composition. Making mistakes is part of the learning process. The most important thing is to not expose our soul and singing voice to unconscious people who project their own demons onto us. The projections can be diabolically subtle, so we must use our animal instinct and watch out for any malevolent tendencies that aim to undermine the musical ground we stand upon. Be careful with people who wrap their criticism in sentences that start with: "For your own good…"

Creative Song Writing

Another way to approach song therapy is to encourage clients to write and compose their own songs. This can be initiated through creative therapeutic writing. By this I mean that clients can initially be encouraged to keep a daily diary of thoughts and images which they write down or paint. It is important to protect these creative treasures since they can inspire musical airs and melodies that their souls resonate with. The words and sentences have their own rhythms and prosody, and to become conscious of this one should vocalize and sound the words so that the ears awaken to these subtle musical nuances. Jung always encouraged the embodied and ensouled "enactment" of dreams, not just an intellectual understanding or obsession with symbol dictionaries. The unconscious appreciates our creative response. Both writing and composing are creative enactments that will be echoed back to us by the unconscious. The unconscious is like nature and often starts guiding the creative process in the most surprising ways. Nature is a master of creation if we but open our eyes to it. Nature is a grand composer if we but listen, surrender, and resonate with her musical callings.

Many of us do not have the best of experiences with words. Words can be very deceiving and can conceal what is really going on in the depths of our psyche. There is however a way out of the shadows of oppressive words if we liberate the words that are alive. Words can become surprisingly wild if we set them free by breaking the bars of professional jargon and psychobabble that imprison them. To enter the wilderness of the poetic and musical world of words, Jungian analyst Russell A. Lockhart suggests that we should treat "words as animals." Digging for the etymological roots of words will often bring surprising revelations. We can search for the active Eros energy in words that moves our souls at a deep level. By focusing more on verbs instead of nouns and adjectives we set things in magic motion. Lockhart is critical of what he calls the "seduction of nouns and adjectives" and he writes:

"The seduction of nouns and adjectives leading into a separatist language, a language in the service of rationality and linearity, insisting on subject-object distinctions. Its aim is distance, its style is prose, its claim is science, its anima is progress: getting somewhere. The language of such separation is made in sentences. But what do sentences sentence us to? Something is imprisoned in the sentence, and it yearns to be free...

But one can get to the eros in words, the animal in words, by discovering the images hidden beneath the shell of words. When you reach this erotic layer in language you begin to experience the poetry in language, the poetry from which words spring, 'poesis,' a fundamental poetry where psyche and the world are one...Playing with the language, and in its deepest sense, 'loving' the language in all the senses of love one can imagine. That way with language would help us to connect with 'the great animals in the background who seem to regulate the world.'"[26]

If we take a non-rational and intimate 'Eros-look' at the word "heart" we can see that within the word "heart" we find three other words: "hear," "ear" and "art." Perhaps this means that we should listen with the ear of the heart if we want to create visionary art. It might also mean that art must come from the heart if it is to be truly soulful and not just a temporary trend or fashion on the market. If we go into anagram mode and move the letter 'h' in heart to the end, we get the word 'earth.' Does this mean that there is a connection between the heart and the earth and art and the ear? Does the earth have an invisible heart whose pulse we can hear if we close our eyes and listen with our animal ears?

This way of playing with words, and falling in love with some of them, can be an inspiration when composing and song writing, and can be a way to liberate the singer within. Composing a song can, of course, also be done the opposite way, i.e., first the tunes and then the words. It is well to remember that composing music does not necessarily begin with theory, and as Zuckerkandl writes:

> *"The scale is not the beginning of music. Figuring out a scale first, then building melodies from the material of the scale: this is not the way music develops.*
> *People sing. Melodies appear. Scales are later theoretical abstractions, the result of reflection about tonal material used in melodies."*[27]

We can listen and pick up tunes in the air or get a little keyboard or guitar or a little rattle and play around. To trust our creative composing and listening skill takes time, but most of us hear musical themes now and then, if we really listen with the ear of our heart. Our dreams can also bring us mysterious tunes and melodies. These tunes should be recorded and kept as a 'sound diary.' Our psyche always responds if we show that we care for what psyche brings to us. It is good to pay attention to the intervals and distances between tones, "our hearing a melody is not a hearing of tones, but 'between' tones – that music occurs not in the tones but between them."[28]

When we have gathered some of our tunes, it is time to listen for words that can fit the music. It is very important to start listening to other composers' music in a new way. We should listen to them as though we are *composers* of music and not *consumers* of music. Being a musical detective is fun. The mind likes to figure things out. How is this verse composed and how does it lead to the chorus? What images and symbols are combined? This way of listening is a revealing voyage. However, start with simple songs and then move on. Remember that a simple and good song is often the hardest to write and compose. It is much easier to hide behind abstractions and over-ambitious complexities.

In song therapeutic work, there is also the dimension of creative writing. Writing a diary, creating stories and poems can lead us into the depths of our musical psyche and composing of songs. Here the ego is not of much use since it often lives in the illusion that it is the sole creator of everything. I suggest instead a more surrendering approach, a surrendering to deep listening so that we can hear what music we already have within us, what tonal worlds are trying to come through. There can be a song inside the story or the poem, and the animal instinct within us can sniff its way to it. In the story we can look for its inherent themes and distil the essence of it. It is in the bones of a story, in its magical marrow, that the song usually resides—waiting for its musical release. Some sculpturers describe their creative work as though they are just assisting in the release of the numinous being residing within the stone. The being, the song, is already there—our job is to get it out of its entrapment and set it free. When doing this we become instruments of archetypal powers, servants of the creative nature of the musical Self. This kind of writing and composing requires a humble attitude and a true trust in the 'feeling response.' Buhner gives us the following guidance on what a true 'feeling response' is:

"It is 'only' because that thing already exists within you that you have the deep feeling response to it, it is part of who you are. And that work of fiction, non-fiction, or poetry moves you 'only' because the depth of meaning that it contains within it is 'already' in you."[29]

Our dreams can, of course, be a great source for our creative writing and composing of songs. Our unconscious is very responsive when we pay attention to the world of psyche. Some people hear evocative words, mysterious sentences, and magical poetry in their dreams, and some also hear songs and music or musical fragments of them. These are gifts from the spirit of the depths and if we record and write down these poetic and musical dream memories the chances are that we will continue receiving more creative visions from the spirits. By just putting a 'dream recorder' at our bedside table will sometimes alert our psyche to recite her poems and sing her songs in our dreams – her calling out to us in the velvet night. It makes a huge difference if we approach our creative acts as though they *really* matter. We should therefore create images and songs as part of our individuation journey and write poems as a way towards freedom. With Jungian analyst Susan Tiberghien's words we should be "writing towards wholeness."[30]

"Imagination is more important than knowledge" said Einstein, "since knowledge is limited and imagination encircles the world."[31] When writing and composing it is in the imagination we must trust. The imagination is *not* a fantasy – the imagination is real. When writing, singing, and painting, it can sometimes feel as though we are dreaming with open eyes, as though the voyage into the imagination alters our state of consciousness. In this altered state of mind, similar to a semi-trance, we come closer to soul and can receive its gifts of beauty. Soul is not only about beauty, but the experience of the numen of pure beauty can be a direct path to the musical gods.

The French philosopher Simone Weil spent her whole life in devotion to transcendent beauty and with profound attention to "waiting for God." She wrote:

"The soul's natural inclination to love beauty is the trap God most frequently uses in order to win it and open it to the breath from on high…
Beauty is the only finality here below…
Every true artist has had a real, direct, and immediate contact with the beauty of the world, a contact that is the nature of a sacrament…
We cannot contemplate without a certain love…
Beauty is eternity here below…
God is pure beauty…
Beauty is always a miracle."[32]

I find it therapeutically important to pay attention to 'beauty' and 'joy' since some of us do not allow ourselves to experience sublime beauty nor do we allow ourselves to express joy. By not expressing our feelings there might be an abundance of repressed laughter and wild playful energy within us. The reason for this could perhaps be that we grew up in depressive environments in which our parents denied us the expression of spontaneous feelings as this can trigger them to feel what they do not want to feel, i.e., to come in touch with their own psychic wounds. If the parents are not willing to become conscious of and take responsibility for their repressed emotions, they will do whatever they can to abuse and silence the child. And, in a similar way, so will unconscious therapists use and silence their clients. As psychoanalyst Alice Miller wrote: "As long as the therapist is not aware of his repression, it can compel him to use his patients, who depend on him, to meet his unmet needs with substitutes."[33]

Another aspect of inner oppression is what can be called the 'perfectionist complex.' This complex is a tricky 'shadow' that in a subtle way tries to convince us that we are not good enough, i.e., not meditating or praying enough, not singing, writing or creating enough, or going to therapy and crying enough. When we are caught up in this complex, we delude ourselves to believe that the gods are not responding to our calls and needs because we are not 'perfect' enough. This is pure diabolical thinking, the devil's voice in disguise and this voice is very seductive. The diabolical voice can convince us that we are listening to the voice of God and in this almighty God's presence laughter is not allowed, instead he should be feared. The book and the film *The Name of the Rose* give an excellent example of the oppressive "spiritual complex" in its most vicious demonic state.[34] It shows how religious dogmatic power figures can hold people trapped by fear and thereby keep them from laughter and life's beauty. These dogmatic and power-ridden figures also live within our psyches.

Repressed feelings of joy and beauty often surface when we liberate our voices and start singing. These expressive sounds show us how important it is to realize that therapy is not only about crying our wounds out. In fact, psychological wounds are like physical wounds. Some wounds need disinfecting and regular deep cleansing before they can heal. On the other hand, some psychological wounds should, just like physical wounds, be left alone and not be constantly torn open. If left alone these wounds will heal by themselves, just like physical wounds. Therapy cannot be a sole means to constantly torture ourselves with sorrowful and painful memories. Therapy must also be about expressively releasing the joy that has been hiding in the shadows.

A creative therapy is about reclaiming the spontaneous inner child and to set it free. The inner child knows sublime beauty and the transcendent path to the gods. We should not repress this spiritual instinct in our inner child. The child loves singing and knows the healing power of music as does the soul. Jung also emphasized the archetypal dimension of the child motif and the mythology of the child gods.

> *"Life is a flux, a flowing into the future, and not a stoppage or a backwash. It is therefore not surprising that so many of the mythological saviours are child gods... the 'child' paves the way for a future change of personality... a mediator, bringer of healing, that is, one who makes whole."*[35]

Remembering that the inner child is a mediator between many dimensions, conscious and unconscious, can be helpful in all creative acts. If we are in a writer's block or feel uninspired in our singing, it is time to reconnect to the fluid transformative energy of the child – personal and archetypal.

People often complain that they are not talented enough for writing song lyrics or for singing. They throw their own creative gifts into the dark shadows since they believe it is their lack of creative genius that will never allow them to write or sing. My experience is that this is not the real problem. We need, of course, to gain a technical mastery of the art if we are to live as professional artists. The real problem, though, is that many of us are unaware of all the oppressive voices within us which hinder our artistic expressions to emerge. The American writer John Gardner, who also taught creative writing, remarked that the "root problems, in other words, are problems of confidence, self-respect, freedom: The writer's demon is imprisoned by the various ghosts in the unconscious."[36]

So, before we even start our work with creative techniques we need to confront and chase out the oppressive ghosts. These ghosts come in many shapes since we all have our individual stories to deal with. Many of us are afraid of having our words or voices judged and shamed and, if we carry traumatic childhood memories of shame, we will do anything to avoid being exposed to this horror again.

Here we must deal with two psychological issues at the same time. One part of our healing process is to embrace the painful memories of shame and express whatever emotions that are necessary for the cathartic release. This expressive emotional release should preferably happen in the presence of a wise witness. The second part of our healing process is to accept that we might get shamed *again* for our writing or singing. But this time, after healing has taken place, we can protect ourselves and we *will* survive the shaming, and we *will* go on writing, and we *will* keep on singing. To master the second part, it is necessary to drop all sentimentality and to let go of all illusions that tell us that we live in a kind and loving world, and everybody will embrace our poems and our songs. *No, they won't!* Some unconscious people may even be provoked and do their best to silence us, especially if the poem or the song reveals them to themselves. They do not want any revelations. They want regressive status quo.

When delivering our art to the collective we must therefore be emotionally prepared and aware of the fact that if our creations "extend awareness further than society wants it to go"[37] we might get shamed by the so-called cultural elite. This shaming can come in many shapes: anything from bad reviews in media or scapegoating or gate blocking or just plain silence. Stephen Harrod Buhner was inspired by Henry Corbin and a great defender of the 'imaginal realm' and wrote that:

"It is our job to reclaim our feeling sense, reclaim the imaginal, to counter the assault on the imaginal realm, on our dreamers, and on the dreamer within us. It is only those who have reclaimed the feeling sense and touch the imaginal who can reliably be trusted to speak truth to power. And it is always the powerful that seek to assault the imaginal for the imaginal is always outside and beyond their control... Those who have access to the imaginal will always see through the surface to what is underneath for they 'feel' what is underneath all surfaces. Automatically. They will never settle for the virtual. Thus, they are, by definition, dangerous."[38]

To quote John Gardner: "To write at all is to lay oneself open to attack, even scorn."[39] As we all know from history, it is the radical writers and the subversive singers who are among the first to be shot when a dictatorial regime takes over. If not all subversive singers and writers are shot, they are silenced through vicious means. Some books are potentially powerful weapons; words can be like swords, the word 'word' lives within the word 'sword'. Jung wrote that "a book can swing even a whole world if it is written in fire and blood."[40] Dictators are very much aware of the swinging sword that is within the power of the word. They know that the sharp edges of a word can sometimes penetrate and cut even deeper if it is sung.

Our fear of the consequences of our creative expressions should be respected as there can be a good reason for our fear. However, if we slowly release some of our fear, a building up of courage can begin. To build up courage is not an easy thing to do, but it is possible and crucial if we want to follow the path of the soul. It is in our hearts we find courage. In French this etymological heart connection is more obvious – 'courage' and 'coeur.' Dorothea Brande's book *Becoming a Writer* is very encouraging for both beginners and professionals in the creative field. With humor and deep compassion, she describes the many pitfalls that creative people can fall into. Her teachings affirm a strong faith in the creative genius of the unconscious, and she advises us to trust and follow its lead when writing.

Living a creative life means to have a certain amount of discipline and a few daily routines. Without this it will be hard to navigate and give shape and form to the gifts and contents of the unconscious. The challenge here is that the unconscious is not overly fond of rules and routines. Sometimes the unconscious can be resistant and make any number of excuses for postponing writing or singing, i.e., we tell ourselves it can wait until tomorrow or next week or next month…or even next year. Brande writes about the wild nature of the unconscious which tries to wriggle itself out of any daily writing discipline, but says that finally, due to our persistence and patience, the "unconscious will suddenly give in charmingly, and begin to write gracefully and well."[41] So, dealing with our creativity is a bit like dealing with a beloved pet. A certain compassionate firmness is required for navigating this instinctual creative field.

Jung writes that "the symbols of the Self arise in the depths of the body… The symbol is thus a living body."[42] Because of this, the flow of creative song writing can sometimes be released by doing other nonverbal body activities. Instead of remaining creatively blocked at our desk it can be liberating to take a break to either paint, dance, or take a nature walk. Movement and dance are powerful creative techniques for getting in touch with the slumbering memories in our bodies and the creative energy of the unconscious. As dancer and dance therapist Anna Halprin writes:

"The experience of movement connected to feelings generates long-buried and unknown emotions and images. When these emotions and images are expressed through movement, we dance. And when

these dances are connected to our lives, they bring about dramatic release and change our will to live."[43]

In whichever way we move, the life enhancing activity we use to free ourselves from our creative blockage, and back into song writing mode, should in a positive sense be quite monotonous and not require any complex thinking. We should feel as though we were moving in a trance-like flow and keep a feeling in the heart that we are dancing ourselves into the unknown poem or song. Jungian analyst and dance therapist Joan Chodorow sees dance and 'authentic movement' as active imaginations and says that if we are deeply present while moving our bodies we can unblock and release the psychic energies that enhance our creativity. Chodorow writes that "the primordial images themselves will lead us to experience the emotion."[44] Therefore, while moving, dancing, or walking, keep a 'memory recorder' close by since the unconscious can bring up images, sounds and words via the body at the most unexpected moments. Make sure to treasure and guard them and bring them close to your soul. Feel them, express them, and turn some of them into art. If you cannot endure this solitary act, find a compassionate and wise witness to support you.

From a more prosaic perspective, I also know of artists who get their best ideas while driving on the highway or standing in the shower or washing the dishes. And, as I wrote earlier, one artistic activity can free another. The poet and painter William Blake realized that the more he painted the more his visionary writing started to come through. The writer Brenda Ueland was very inspired by Blake's art and wrote that he made her realize that human creativity is divine and given to us by God. She wrote that "this creative power I think is the Holy Ghost... it is life itself. It is the Spirit. In fact, it is the only important thing about us."[45]

If we feel that our creative ideas and visions are coming from a divine power, then we must devote ourselves to them. We must stay centered in our hearts while lovingly working with our music and poetry. This spiritual approach gives dignity to our creations. Song writing can then be a way to unveil the mystery of the soul, a musical voyage to reveal hidden treasures in the land of psyche. Deena Metzger works with creative story writing as a healing tool and says:

> *"Every activity of the creative process requires that we bring spirit into form, that we create a vessel – ourselves or a work of art – that can hold the spirit. Lover or demon, invited or feared, the muse can transmit the energy that enlivens our work…The muse is the guardian angel or the daimon of our creativity."*[46]

To "bring spirit into form" requires attention and time and place for solitude. Some of us find it difficult to be alone with ourselves since in our solitude we might have to face ourselves, something we might not be ready for. One of the challenges for an artist is to avoid distractions and interruptions. Even the slightest little disturbance can disrupt our creative flow as it will take us out of our writing trance. And once we are brought out of this trance it is hard to re-enter our creative flow again. The disruptions feel as though we have been abruptly woken up from a dream causing the dream images to slip down like seals into the water again, disappearing back into the depths of the ocean of dreams. I know of one writer who refused to answer the phone when she was writing since she felt that just one phone call in the morning could disrupt her creative flow for the entire day.

It is from the unconscious we receive the creative gifts, and the unconscious is very sensitive to how we treat what has been given us, as are the gods. We know that the dreaming psyche is not content with merely intellectual dream interpretations. For dreams to be transformative we need to take ethical and creative action on the messages we get from our dreams. If, for example, the dream instructs us to paint with the colour purple, then with purple we must paint. We cannot just ponder passively over what 'paint' and 'purple' might mean 'symbolically.' The unconscious demands of the artist to take its visions seriously, and I mean *seriously*. It is not enough to just be slightly 'interested' since this does not resonate deep enough with musical psyche. When psyche sings her songs to us, we must be totally devoted to her callings. If we constantly distract ourselves with all kinds of trivialities and still expect the gods to deliver their golden gifts, then we are on the wrong path and the unconscious will sooner or later withhold her gifts.

"God, according to scripture, does not come with the noise of wrathfulness but as imperceptibly as a breeze." Songs are not only about sound, songs are also about silence – deep silence at certain numinous moments. The philosopher and musicologist Vladimir Jankélévitch writes about the subtle "charme" of some music, the sense of a numinous poetic grace and he means that "music renews its strength at the fountain of silence."[47] In solitude and in silence is where renewal and transformation can take place, and where something Other and sublime can enter. In silence we can open the ear of our heart to the song of the soul. In silence our auditory perception can sense the vibrations of the music of the imaginal realm.

> *"Supersensory voices and infrasensory voices are something else entirely, of an entirely other sonic order than the noises of the day. Just as clairvoyants, or those endowed with superhuman sight, see in darkness – with second sight (which is intuition) – and see invisible essences hidden behind that which exists visibly, so silence allows a kind of 'second hearing' to develop, aural finesse, which allows human beings to perceive the least murmur of wind and night. Silence is a good conductor: it transmits implications hidden within what we can and do hear and allows a universal mystery and its voices to approach human beings."*[48]

Sounding The Mana

In my Song Therapy courses I use and teach specific vocal techniques that embrace a wide spectrum of sounds and timbres. Some of these techniques in Voice Movement Therapy I learned from Paul Newham while training at the Royal Society of Arts in London 1997-1998. Since then, I have transformed and fine-tuned them, so they now suit my therapeutic and artistic vision of psyche, sound, and song. This song-therapeutic voyage touches both upon the archetypal and personal spheres and can have a profound cathartic effect. The healing has nothing to do with volume and loudness, it is not that difficult to be loud, though sometimes a primal sound can be a salvation. Instead, the psychospiritual transformation happens when we become profoundly present in the sound, or the *duende* of the silence. Once we become present in our songs we must try to feel and express the emotions that rise within us when we sing. It is in this emotional release that healing can take place. Just making sounds leads to nothing more than just sound-making. Instead, we must come home to the sound and release whatever keeps us from this. To liberate our voice is to liberate our psyche. To free the sound is to free the soul. Music is a magical magnet, a sacred gift from Mnemosyne and the Muses, who free our voices so that our songs can sound the Mana of the Mysterion.

It is liberating to embrace all the energy and emotions that surface during this musical soul journey. The sounds and movements can reach both developmental and archetypal levels of psyche. Sometimes we feel resistance when a song brings up painful memories from the past. By befriending this resistance and thereby emotionally moving through it, we can feel how our voices and vocal sounds start to open. Numinous energy can enter us in this expressive act, and through singing we draw nearer to the gods.

The human collective has invented a reward system that consists of a great many points for the upward journey – in alignment with the eagle, the sun, and the sky, and in denial of the earth and the serpent. We get good degrees when we acquire advanced philosophical thinking skills, verbal complexity, advanced language efficiency as well as calculation and speculation abilities. Some of us believe that spiritual power resides only in heaven and nowhere else. Why would they otherwise stretch their arms – like wings – towards the vast skies when making a gesture to the so-called spiritual dimension. I do not mean that there is anything wrong in reaching for the sky, nothing wrong with being up there in those lofty spheres – it is alright as long we do not get stuck up there.

Another interesting phenomenon here is that some of us tend to stand on our toes, as though wanting to transcend gravity and leave earth, just to hit a high tone. High tones are often collectively encouraged and associated with a religious dimension, but there is no connection whatsoever with high tones and heaven, or even God, for that matter. A high tone is not even high – we just use spatial concepts to describe the tonal land. In reality, it is the speed by which the vocal folds vibrate which determines how we experience the musical tones, i.e., high speed: high tones, slow speed: low tones. It is all about frequencies.

As children we are encouraged by enthusiastic parents when we ascend and rise from all fours and stop crawling on the floor. We are also rewarded when we use our contracting skills by not screaming and giving sounds in all directions. Slowly but progressively the floor becomes our enemy and for some adults to fall over and land on the floor can feel like the end of the world. The collective ideal of living in a constant state of ascent and controlled contraction has gone so far that it one-sidedly occupies our whole collective concept of what is intelligent and what is not.

I believe we have mistaken the straight standing 'homo erectus' knowledge for sacred wisdom. It is as though the more we leave the instinctual animal in us behind, the more we believe we have acquired a great cultural value. Still, when we look into the eyes of an animal, we sense something vast and mysterious, and at least a part of us is aware that this dark mystery – this *lumen naturae* – holds a sublime light. This divine light can guide us back when we have deviated too far from our instincts – too far from our souls and songs.

When working with clients, I often witness the struggle involved in being willing to let go of a tight throat, a highly articulate tongue, stiff lips, and being overly smart and sharp. Singing – the opening of one's vocal tract – is a contrary movement to the collective's ideal of upward-striving and tight contraction. Giving ourselves permission to vocalize instinctual sounds once again can therefore bring up very strong emotions in the so-called 'well behaved'. Some feel immature and un-intelligent, and this can be experienced as an act that will attract punishment or ridicule – it is a journey into the Other. Our culture generally encourages women to sing in high-pitched voices and men in low-pitched voices. Clients who dare to transgress this sometimes report afterwards that it felt as though it was someone else giving sound. They say this with mixed feelings as they often feel both a certain tickling pleasure and a slight trembling fear when encountering the sound of the anima and the animus in their voice. By psychologically embracing and vocally expressing the various vocal timbres – the whole spectrum of sounds – we reclaim all our selves and can sing for wholeness.

Even though we all have our own unique and individual voices, our voices are much more flexible than we usually imagine. Sometimes I envision the voice journey as covering the vast spatial distance between the eagle and the serpent. To keep our singing voices flexible none of these symbolic animals should be favoured more than the other. The two different elements these animals have had to master have forced them to develop unique surviving skills in accordance with the nature of each element. The voice also needs specific skills to navigate different elements. The eagle knows the spirit of the wind and the fiery power of the sun. The serpent knows the soul of the earth and the cleansing transcendence of water. These animals are good judges of knowing exactly when the right moment has arrived – the moment of *Kairos*. They are excellent at timing – they know when to hesitate, they know when to accelerate, can instantly measure distances and with their full attention wait until it is time to strike. Accurate timing is of the utmost importance in the world of music. We can in no way get any response from a sensitive and conscious audience if the musical timing is not precise. Exact timing is also crucial in all therapeutical professions. The serpent and the eagle know how to use this instinctual archetypal knowledge with extreme precision. Like all animals, they also know how to fully live who they are meant to be – in harmonic resonance with their fates.

If we dim the light and imagine an eagle's head in profile, as though we are in a dream state, it resembles the head of a serpent, and from a deeper perspective they can be one. There are also mythic images of them becoming one being. An example of this is found in the Mesoamerican mythology – Quetzalcoatl, the winged serpent. What I have described here is of course only one aspect of the singer's journey – the vibrating vertical serpent-eagle spiral. If the singer is at home with the soul in the body, singing starts a psychological process that can reach down to the darkest depths and way up to the brightest heights.

The human voice can only cover the stretch that the psyche is able to fathom, i.e., we can only sing in accordance with our emotional state and how much archetypal energy our soul is able to receive and channel from the Self. The psychological and physical challenge is to try to hold this energy while simultaneously being in contact with Eros and relating to the audience.

This can be seen as a symbolical earth and sky enactment. As singers we must ground ourselves deeply in the earth, in alignment with the serpent, if we with our voices want to reach the sky where the eagle soars. I believe that the Greek images of Hermes with his wings and a serpent staff, of Asclepios with his serpents and dogs, and Orpheus surrounded by all the creatures of the animal kingdom, hint at this necessary alignment with our instincts if therapy and music is to bring healing. It is in resonating empathy and deep sympathy that real emotional and spiritual transformation can take place.

To liberate the voice and connect our soul and heart to the song can for some of us feel like an archetypal musical experience of tasting the mythological forbidden fruit. Soulful singing is achieved through the support of the bodily centers, so from a symbolical perspective it is impossible for us to refuse the serpent's temptation if we want to sing with our whole body and soul. Or, it would be better to say that the musical gift of the serpent and the eagle opens us so that our soul and body can be sung through by the spirit of both depth and of height.

I remember Jungian analyst Marion Woodman once telling me in a workshop in Einsiedeln that "in those brief moments when we do manage to free our authentic voices, the whole being resonates with that truth and at that numinous moment there is a marriage of the personal and the transpersonal."[49]

To be able to guide someone safely in a song therapy session or in a Jungian analytic session requires presence and attention. I would say we have a lot to learn from the animals about this musical art and therapeutic skill. I cannot recall ever having met a human who has been as profoundly present as my dogs. Therefore, I sometimes allow myself to envision a future where animals are being invited as numinous attention-teachers at schools and training institutes. It would probably be a bit chaotic in the beginning, but there could emerge a hidden divine order on the instinctual level. We could furthermore open each lecture by rhythmically reciting the words of philosopher Simone Weil: *Attention is the rarest and purest form of generosity.*[50]

ENDNOTES

[1] Anne M. Brownell, Deirdre A. Brownell, Gina Holloway Mulder (editors), *Singing the Psyche – Uniting Thought and Feeling through the Voice (Voice Movement Therapy in Practice)*, Charles C. Thomas Publisher Ltd, 2023, p. xvii.

[2] Paul Newham, lecture, Voice Movement Therapy Training, Royal Society of Arts, London, 1997.

[3] Shaun McNiff, *The Arts and Psychotherapy*, Charles C. Thomas Publisher, 1981, p. xv.

[4] Victor Zuckerkandl, *Man the Musician*, Princeton University Press, Bollingen Series, transl. Norbert Guterman, 1976, p. 7 - 8.

[5] For more information on song therapy see www.lenamandotter.com

[6] Donald Kalshed, *Trauma and the Soul*, Routledge, 2013.

[7] Victor Zuckerkandl, *The Sense of Music*, p. 4 and 12.

[8] Diane Austin, *The Theory and Practice of Vocal Psychotherapy – Songs of the Self*, Jessica Kingsley Publishers, 2008, p. 136.

[9] For more journeys to release the wild voice see Caitlín Matthews, *Singing the Soul Back Home*, Element Books, 1995.

[10] For information on scientific research on the heart, see Heartmath Institute's website, and the books by Stephen Harrod Buhner, *The Secret Teachings of Plants* and *Plant Intelligence and the Imaginal Realm*, Paula Reeves, *Heart Sense,* and Anne Elizabeth Taylor, *Unveiling Sophia – Heart Wisdom in an Age of Technology*.

[11] Stephen Harrod Buhner, *Plant Intelligence and the Imaginal Realm*, Bear & Company, 2014, p. 508.

[12] Carl Gustav Jung, *Nietzsche Zarathustra Seminar*, p. 757.

[13] Carl Gustav Jung, Collected Works Vol. 8, *The Structure and Dynamics of the Psyche*, p. 86.

14 Carl Gustav Jung, Collected Works Vol. 8, p. 204.

15 The Holy Bible, John 1 and Genesis 1:3.

16 Russell A. Lockhart, *Words as Eggs – Psyche in Language and Clinic*, The Lockhart Press, 2012, Original printing: Spring Journal 1983, p. 92.

17 Juliet Miller, *The Creative Feminine and Her Discontents – Psychotherapy, Art and Destruction*, Karnac Books, 2008, p. 20.

18 Diane Cousineau Brutsche, *Lady Soul*, ed. Murray Stein/ Nancy Cater, *The Symbolic Life*, Spring Journal vol. 82, 2009, p. 103 and 109.

19 Hazrat Inayat Khan, *The Mysticism of Music, Sound and Word*, The Sufi Message Vol. 2, Motilal Banarsidass, 1988, pp. 164 - 165 and p. 185.

20 Clarissa Pinkola Estés, *Women Who Run with the Wolves*, Rider/Random House, 1998, p. 24.

21 Joel Kroeker, *Jungian Music Psychotherapy – When Psyche Sings*, Routledge, 2019, p. 68.

22 Blaise Pascal, *Pensées*, Wikipedia

23 Carl Gustav Jung, *Dreams*, Princeton University Press, Bollingen Series, 2010 (origin. 1974), transl. R.F.C. Hull, p. 80.

24 Patricia Skar, *The Matrix of Music and Analysis*, ed. P. Ashton & S. Bloch, *Music and Psyche*, p. 90.

25 Carl Gustav Jung, *Dreams*, p. 136.

26 Russell A. Lockhart, *Psyche* Speaks – *a Jungian Approach to Self and World*, Chiron Publications, 1987, p. 85 - 86. (last sentence in quote is by C.G. Jung, *Letters*, p. 605)

27 Victor Zuckerkandl, *The Sense of Music*, p. 25.

28 Ibid., p. 30.

29 Stephen Harrod Buhner, *Ensouling Language – On the Art of Non-Fiction and the Writer's life*, p. 73.

30 Susan M. Tiberghien, *Writing Towards Wholeness – Lessons inspired by C.G. Jung*, Chiron Publications, 2018.

31 www.goodreads.com

32 Simone Weil, *Waiting for God*, Harper & Row Publishers, 1973 (origin. 1951, G P Putnam's Sons), p.163 - 172 and p. 213.

33 Alice Miller, *The Drama of Being a Child – The Search for the True Self*, (revised and updated version), transl. Ruth Ward, Virago, 2008, p. 10.

[34] Umberto Eco, *The Name of the Rose*, Harcourt, 1983 and film adaptation by Jean-Jacques Annaud, 1986.

[35] Carl Gustav Jung and Karl Kerényi, *Essays on a Science of Mythology*, p. 83.

[36] John Gardner's foreword to Dorothea Brande's book, *Becoming a Writer*, Jerome P Tarcher/Putnam, 1981, p. 12.

[37] Stephen Harrod Buhner, *Ensouling Language – On the Art of Non-Fiction and the Writer's Life*, p. 373.

[38] Ibid., p. 373.

[39] John Gardner's foreword to Dorothea Brande's book, *Becoming a Writer*, Jerome P. Tarcher/Putnam, 1981, p. 12 and p. 14.

[40] Carl Gustav Jung, *The Red Book*, p. 130, note 44.

[41] Ibid., p. 79.

[42] Carl Gustav Jung, *The Archetypes and the Collective Unconscious,* Collected Works, Vol. 9, part 1, Routledge & Kegan Paul, 1971, p. 173.

[43] Anna Halprin, *Returning to Health with Dance, Movement and Imagery*, Life Rhythm, 2002, p. 13.

[44] Joan Chodorow, *Dance Therapy & Depth Psychology – the Moving Imagination*, Routledge, 2008, p. 134.

[45] Brenda Ueland, *If You Want to Write – a Book about Art, Independence and Spirit*, Greywolf Press, 1987, p. 10.

[46] Deena Metzger, *Writing for Your Life – a Guide and Companion to the Inner Worlds*, 1992, Harper San Francisco, p. 188.

[47] Vladimir Jankélévitch, *Music and the Ineffable*, Princeton University Press, 2003, transl. Carolyn Abbate, p. 149 - 153.

[48] Ibid., p. 153.

[49] Marion Woodman, *BodySoul Rhythms*, workshop in Einsiedeln Switzerland, 2008.

[50] Simone Weil, *Letter to Joe Bousquet*, 13 April, 1942, Simone Pétrement, *Simone Weil: A Life*, Pantheon Books, 1976, p. 462.

THE SONG OF THE SOUL
Postlude

Jung pointed out that music mirrors the movements, motifs, and patterns of the archetypal powers. Since songs can be therapeutic and alchemical vessels for both personal emotions and objective psychic energies, Jung proposed that music should be an essential part of psychoanalysis since it reaches those depths of our psyche that the 'talking cure' may not reach.

I have resonated with the words of Jung and made a musical circumambulation – a voyage into the archetypal dimension of sound and song. My focus has been on song more than music since the human voice is the only musical instrument that is sounded from within our body and soul. Generally, I believe in music therapy too with its many inventive approaches, but in my own song therapy I prefer to work voice to voice, song to song, and soul to soul with no other musical accompaniment than the voice and the song of the other.

Being guided towards the archetypal world of song, I have engaged with soul, breath, and spirit. The archetypal themes of the numinous winds moved me to Lorca's poetic concept of *duende* and Corbin's vision of the *imaginal* realm – a transpersonal dimension – a space for artistic and soulful alchemical transformation. There I entered communion with Hermes, the very first archetypal musician – the musical messenger between gods and humans. After having felt the wild wings of his being, I then landed on Earth and joined the animals, finding a reconciling force of spirit and instinct in the shamanic musician Orpheus.

The song of the soul can touch and hold our deepest joys and darkest sorrows and is therefore a musical agent for healing. The song can aid us both as a guide to our wounds and as a vibrating vessel for psychic transformation. In deep song, we often feel the archetypal dimension that brings us into communion with the Self. We must therefore humbly honor and surrender to the potential value of song and art. These are the final questions by film director Andrey Tarkovsky about the surrendering act into the mystery of art:

> "...one thing that mankind has ever created in a spirit of self-surrender is the artistic image. Perhaps the meaning of all human activity lies in artistic consciousness... (in the) selfless creative act? Perhaps our capacity to create is evidence that we ourselves were created in the image and likeness of God?"[1]

The best way to communicate the mystery of soul and song would be to sing, says my singer within, and I truly believe her. On the other hand, if our words can be soulfully "inhabited"; if our words and writing can follow numinous golden strings and move us into musical dream time, then I as a singer will be sounding along.[2] But still, the song of the soul can *never* be entirely explained. The song belongs to the ineffable realm and will remain a mystery which is one of its true blessings.

When Jung was asked about the meaning of love, he always remained silent because he knew that he was asked about a mystery too deep to fathom – a transcendent "cosmogonic god." When the virtuoso cello player Paul Tortelier was asked how he felt about teaching cello, he answered that it was not only about music, but also about love.[3] So, it seems that the gods and love and music are intimately related, and that song can be the vehicle into the imaginal realm where this divine union of Eros and music can be experienced.

This book has mainly focused on the archetypal dimension of song, but of course, a song can also be a musical vessel for the personal dimension. My reason for illuminating the archetypal dimension is because the archetypal touch can bring such deep and sometimes instantaneous healing. This can be compared to the transformative power of visions or the 'big' dreams we on rare occasions are gifted in the night. Jungian analyst Andreas Schweizer emphasizes this archetypal effect in his book about the Egyptian sungod's journey. He writes that "even today, it happens that the entire course of a person's life is changed by a single dream or visionary image. When someone is touched by the numinous, it leaves deep traces."[4]

There is a world beyond therapy and, as a singer and song-therapist, I therefore listen and relate to the song as a healer in itself—an alchemical musical vessel for transformation. As professor Shaun McNiff writes about art and healing: "The medicinal agent is art itself, which releases and contains psyche's therapeutic forces."[5]

And now I will leave you here at the singing crossroads. It is a good place to be if we can bear the unknown – the liminal nonverbal sound-space – awaiting the birth of the light leading to a new dawn of songs. Something will sooner or later move and lead us on. Something much stronger than ourselves – a loving musical force that is awaiting us if we but dare to trust the song of our soul. I leave you here in silence, with some lyrical words by Henry Corbin about the mystery of soul, song, and music.

"The human voice then appears…
and finally culminating in its own climax of pathos,
and then progressively re-descends towards silence.
And then comes the conclusion,
with the instrument accompanying this silence,
finally seeming to lose itself like arpeggios of a distant light,
that light in which the mystic awaits the new dawn."[6]

ENDNOTES

[1] Andrey Tarkovsky, *Sculpting in Time – Reflections on the Cinema*, University of Texas Press, 2010, p. 241. and film seminars with Jungian analyst and film director Ingela Romare.

[2] Stephen Harrod Buhner, *Ensouling Language,* Inner Traditions, 2010.

[3] Jungian analyst and film director Peter Ammann's film about cellist Paul Tortelier, *The Complete Musician*, VAI.

[4] Andreas Schweizer, *The Sungod's Journey through the Netherworld*, Cornell University Press, 2010, p. 14.

[5] Shaun McNiff, *Art as Medicine – Creating a Therapy of the Imagination*, Shambhala Publications, 1992, p. 3.

[6] Henry Corbin, *The Voyage and the Messenger*, p. 234.

BIBLIOGRAPHY, BOOKS, FILMS, MUSIC-ALBUMS

Abram, David, *The Spell of the Sensuous – Perception and Language in a More-Than-Human World*, Vintage Books/Random House, 1997.

Abram, David, *Becoming Animal – an Earthly Cosmology*, Pantheon Books, 2010.

Achterberg, Jeanne, *Imagery in Healing – Shamanism and Modern Medicine*, Shambhala Publications, 1985.

Ammann, Peter, *The Complete Musician*, a film about cellist Paul Tortelier. VAI, 2014.

Ammann, Peter, *The Spirit of the Rocks*, Triluna Film AG, 2002.

Ashton P. W. and Bloch S., ed., *Music and Psyche,* Spring Journal Books, 2010.

Athanassakis, Apostolos and Wolkow, Benjamin, *The Orphic Hymns*, John Hopkins University Press, 2013.

Austin, Diane, *The Theory and Practice of Vocal Psychotherapy – Songs of the Self*, Jessica Kingsley Publishers, 2008.

Bachelard, Gaston, *On Poetic Imagination and Reverie*, Spring Publications, 2014.

Berendt, Joachim-Ernst, *The World is Sound, Nada Brahma – Music and the Landscape of Consciousness*, Destiny Books/Inner Traditions, 1991.

Brande, Dorothea, *Becoming a Writer*, Jeremy P Tarcher /Putnam, 1981. (Origin. 1934).

Brook, Peter, *There are No Secrets – Thoughts on Acting and Theatre*, Methuen Drama, 1995.

Brown, Norman, *Hermes the Thief – The Evolution of a Myth*, Random House, 1969.

Brownell, Anne M., ed., *Singing the Psyche – Uniting Thought and Feeling through the Voice (Voice Movement Therapy in Practise)*, co-ed. Gina Holloway Mulder and Deirdre A Brownell. Charles C Thomas Publisher, 2023.

Brutsche, Paul, *Creativity – Patterns of Creative Imagination as Seen Through Art*, Spring Journal Books, 2018.

Buhner, Stephen Harrod, *Plant Intelligence and the Imaginal Realm*, Bear & Company, 2014.

Buhner, Stephen Harrod, *Ensouling Language – On the Art of Non-Fiction and the Writer's Life*, Inner Traditions, 2010.

Buhner, Stephen Harrod, *The Secret Teachings of Plants - The Intelligence of the Heart in Direct Perceiving of Nature*, Bear & Company, 2004.

Caspari, Elisabeth/ Robbins Ken, *Animal Life in Nature, Myth and Dreams*, Chiron Publications., 2003.

Chatwin, Bruce, *The Songlines*, Penguin Books, 1988.

Chodorow, Joan, *Dance Therapy & Depth Psychology – the Moving Imagination*, Routledge, 2008.

Corbin, Henry, *Alone with the Alone: Creative imagination in the Sufism of Ibn 'Arabi*, Princeton University Press, Bollingen Series, 1997.

Corbin, Henry, *Spiritual Body and Celestial Earth*, Princeton University Press, Bolllingen Series, 1989.

Corbin, Henry, *Swedenborg and Esoteric Islam*, Swedenborg Foundation, 2014.

Corbin, Henry, *The Voyage and the Messenger*, North Atlantic Books, 1998.

Corbin, Henry, *Jung, Buddhism and the Incarnation of Sophia*, Inner Traditions, 2019.

Corbin, Henry, *The Man of Light in Iranian Sufism*, Omega Publications, 1994.

Corbin, Henry, *Temple and Contemplation*, Routledge, 2013.

Corbin, Henry, *Avicenna and the Visionary Recital*, Princeton University Press, 1990.

Corbin, Henry, *The Realism and Symbolism of Colors in Shiite Cosmology*, Essay in the Eranos Year Book *Color Symbolism*, Ed. Klaus Ottmann, Spring Publications, 2005.

Cousineau-Brutsche, Diane, *Lady Soul*, essay in *The Symbolic Life*, Spring Journal Vol. 82, 2009.

Davies, James, *Cracked – Why Psychiatry is Doing More Harm than Good*, Icon Books Ltd, 2014.

Davies, James, *Sedated – How Modern Capitalism Created Our Mental Health Crisis*, Atlantic Books, 2022.

Dodds, E R., *The Greeks and the Irrational*, University of California Press, 1951.

Dunn, Patrick, *The Orphic Hymns – A New Translation for the Occult Practitioner*, Llewellyn Publications, 2022.

Eco, Umberto, *The Name of the Rose*, Harcourt, 1983.

Eliade, Mircea, *Shamanism – Archaic Techniques of Ecstasy*, Transl. Willard R Trask, Princeton University Press, Bollingen Series, 1992. (Original 1951)

Eliade, Mircea, *Rites and Symbols of Initiation*, Spring Publications., 2009.

Evetts-Secker, Josephine, *At Home in the Language of the Soul – Exploring Jungian Discourse and Psyche's Grammar of Transformation*, Spring Journal Books, 2012.

Faivre, Antoine, *The Eternal Hermes – from Greek God to Alchemical Magus*, Transl. Godwin, Joscelyn, Phanes Press, 1995.

Frances, Allen, *Saving Normal – An Insider's Revolt Against Out-of-Control Psychiatric Diagnosis, DSM-5, Big Pharma, and the Medicalization of Ordinary Life*, William Morrow/ Harper Collins Publishers, 2013.

Gardner, Howard, *The Arts and Human Development – A Psychological Study of the Artistic Process*, Basic Books, 1994.

Gardner, John, Foreword, Brande, D., *Becoming a Writer*, Jeremy P Tarcher /Putnam, 1981.

Godwin, Joscelyn, *Harmonies of Heaven and Earth*, Inner Traditions, 1995.

Grimm, Jacob/Wilhelm, *The Grimm's Fairytales*, Pantheon Books, 1972.

Grotowski, Jerzy, *Towards a Poor Theatre*, Methuen, 1981.

Guthrie, W K C., *Orpheus and Greek Religion*, Princeton University Press, 1993.

Halprin, Anna, *Returning to Health with Dance, Movement and Imagery*, (a revised version of *Dance as a Healing Art*), Life Rhythm, 2002.

Han, Byung-Chul, *The Disappearance of Rituals – a Topology of the Present*, Polity Press, 2020.

Hannah, Barbara, *The Archetypal Symbolism of Animals*, Chiron Publications, 2006.

Harner, Michael, *The Way of the Shaman*, Harper & Row Publishers, 1990.

Henderson, Joseph and Oakes, Maud, *The Wisdom of the Serpent*, Princeton University Press, 1991.

Ingerman, Sandra, *Soul Retrieval – Mending the Fragmented Self*, Harper SanFrancisco, 1991.

Ingerman, Sandra and Wesselman, Hank (ed.), *Awakening to the Spirit World – The Shamanic Path to Direct Revelation,* Sounds True, 2010.

Jacoby, Mario, *Shame and the Origins of Self-Esteem*, Transl. Douglas Witcher, Routledge, 1996.

Jacoby, Mario, *Jungian Psychotherapy & Contemporary Infant Research,* Routledge, 1999.

Jacoby, Mario, *The Analytic Encounter*, Inner City Books, 1984.

Jankélévitch, Vladimir, *Music and the Ineffable*, Princeton University Press, 2003.

Jenny, Hans, *Cymatics – A Study of Wave Phenomena and Vibration*. Vol 1 & 2 New Rev. Ed. MACROmedia Publishing, 2023.

Jung, Carl Gustav, *Symbols of Transformation*, Collected Works Vol. 5, Princeton University Press, 1956.

Jung, Carl Gustav, *The Red Book (Liber Novus)*, ed. Sonu Shamdasani, The Foundation of the Works of C.G. Jung. W. W. Norton & Company, Philemon Foundation. 2009.

Jung, Carl Gustav, *The Red Book – Liber Novus*, A Reader's Edition, ed. Sonu Shamdasani, transl. Mark Kyburz, John Peck and Sonu Shamdasani, The Foundation of the Works of C.G. Jung, W. W. Norton & Company, 2009. Philemon Series.

Jung, Carl Gustav, *The Art of CG Jung*, ed. The Foundation of the Works of C.G. Jung, W.W. Norton & Company, 2019.

Jung, Carl Gustav, ed. Aniela Jaffé, *Memories, Dreams, Reflections,* Vintage Books/ Random House, 1989.

Jung, Carl Gustav, *Letters – Volume 1*, ed. Gerhard Adler/Aniela Jaffé, Routledge, 1973.

Jung, Carl Gustav, Letters – Volume 2, ed. Gerhard Adler/Aniela Jaffé, Routledge, 1990.

Jung, Carl Gustav, *Selected Letters of C.G. Jung 1909 – 1961*, ed. Gerhard Adler/Aniela Jaffé, Princeton University Press, 1984.

Jung, Carl Gustav, ed. William McGuire & R F C Hull, *C.G. Jung Speaking*, Princeton University Press, 1993.

Jung, Carl Gustav and Kerényi, Karl. *Essays on a Science of Mythology*, Princeton University Press, 1969.

Jung, Carl Gustav, *Childrens Dreams – Notes on the Seminars given 1936 - 1940*, Princeton University Press, 2008.

Jung, Carl Gustav, *Nietzsche Zarathustra Seminar Vol 1 and Vol. 2*, Princeton University Press, 1988.

Jung, Carl Gustav, *Psychological Types Collected Works Vol. 6*, Princeton University Press, 1971.

Jung, Carl Gustav, *The Structure and Dynamics of the Psyche*, Collected Works Vol. 8, transl. R..F.C. Hull, 2nd Edition, Routledge, 2002. (orig. 1960)

Jung, Carl Gustav, *Alchemical Studies*, Collected Works Vol. 13, Princeton University Press, 1983, 3rd print.

Jung, Carl Gustav, *Man and His Symbols*, Dell Publishing, 1968.

Jung, Carl Gustav, ed. Aniela Jaffe, *Word and Image*, Princeton University Press, 1983.

Jung, Carl Gustav, *Visions*, Spring Publications, 1976.

Jung, Carl Gustav, *Dreams,* Princeton University Press, Transl. R.F..C Hull, Bollingen Series, 2010, Origin. 1974.

Jung, Carl Gustav, *The Archetypes and the Collective Unconscious*, Collected Works Vol. 9 part 1, transl. R.F..C Hull, ed. W. McGuire, H. Read, M Fordham, G. Adler, Routledge & Kegan Paul, 2nd ed., third printing, 1971.

Jung, Emma, *Animus and Anima*, Spring Publications, 2008.

The Homeric Hymns, "Hymn to Hermes" nr 4 and 18, Oxford University Press, 2008.

Kalshed, Donald, *Trauma and the Soul*, Routledge, 2013.

Kerényi, Karl, *Asclepios – Archetypal Image of the Physician's Existence*, Thames and Hudson (Bollingen Foundation), 1959., transl. Ralph Mannheim.

Kerényi, Karl, *Hermes – Guide of Souls*, Spring Publications, transl. Murray Stein 2009.

Kerényi, Karl, *The Religion of the Greeks and the Romans*, Thames and Hudson, 1962.

Khan, Hazrat Inayat, *The Mysticism of Music, Sound and Word*, The Sufi Message vol. 2/ Motilal Banarsidass, 1988.

Khan, Hazrat Inayat. *The Music of Life*, Omega Publications, 1983.

Kingsley, Peter, *In the Dark Places of Wisdom,* The Golden Sufi Center, 2010.

Kittelson, Mary Lynn, *Sounding the Soul – The Art of Listening*, Daimon Verlag, 1995.

Kreinheder, Albert, *Body and Soul – the Other Side of Illness*, Inner City Books, 2009.

Krieger, Nancy, *Bridges to Consciousness – Complexes and Complexity*, Routledge, 2014.

Kroeker, Joel, Jungian *Music Psychotherapy – When Psyche Sings,* Routledge, 2019.

Lachman, Gary, *Lost Knowledge of the Imagination*, Floris Books, 2020.

Langer, Susanne K., *Philosophy in a New Key – A Study in the Symbolism of Reason, Rite, and Art*, Harvard University Press, 1957.

Langer, Susanne K., *Feeling and Form – A Theory of Art*, Charles Scribner's Sons, 1953.

Lauterwasser, Alexander, *Water Sound Images – The Creative Music of the Universe*, MACROmedia Publishing, 2006.

Le Brun, Annie, *Reality Overload – the Modern World's Assault on the Imaginal Realm*, Inner Traditions, 2008.

Lewis, Penny, *Creative Transformation – The Healing Power of the Arts*, Chiron Publications, 1993.

Lockhart, Russell A., *Words as Eggs – Psyche in Language and Clinic*, Lockhart Press, 2012. Original Printing; Spring Publications 1983.

Lockhart, Russell A., *Psyche Speaks – a Jungian approach to Self and World*, Chiron Publications, 1987.

Lockhart, Russell A. and Mitchell, Paco, *Dreams, Bones & the Future*, Owl & Heron Press, 2015.

Lockhart Russell A, *Silver, Change, Imagination*, pdf essay at Lockhart's website.

Lopéz Pedraza, Rafael, *Hermes and His Children*, Daimon Verlag, 2010.

Lorca, Federico Garcia, *In Search of Duende*, New Direction Books, 1998.

Mannes, Elena, *The Power of Music – Pioneering Discoveries in the New Science of Song*, Walker Publishing Company, 2011.

Matthews, Caitlín, *Singing the Soul Back Home*, Element Books, 1995.

McNiff, Shaun, *The Arts and Psychotherapy*, Charles C Thomas Publisher, 1981.

McNiff, Shaun, *Art as Medicine – Creating a Therapy of the Imagination*, Shambhala Publications, 1992.

Meier, C A., *Healing Dream and Ritual – Ancient Incubation and Modern Psychotherapy*, Daimon Verlag, 1989.

Metzger, Deena, *Writing for Your Life – a Guide and Companion to the Inner Worlds*, Harper San Francisco, 1992.

Miller, Alice, *The Drama of Being a Child – The Search for the True Self*, (Revised and updated version), transl. Ruth Ward, Virago, 2008.

Miller, Juliet, *The Creative Feminine and Her Discontents – Psychotherapy, Art and Destruction*, Karnac Books, 2008.

Måndotter, Lena, *Prayers & Prophecies – Live at the Palladium*, Kameleont Production, 2017.

Måndotter, Lena, *Live at the Cathedral*, Kameleont Production, 2015.

Måndotter, Lena, *Vysotskij – I Minne*, Kameleont Production, 2015.

Måndotter, Lena, *The Way to the Rose*, Rootsy/Warner Music, 2013.

Måndotter, Lena, *Songs From the River*, Rootsy/Warner Music. 2009.

Måndotter Lena, *Songs of Leonard Cohen*, Rootsy/Warner Music, 2008.

Måndotter, Lena *Songs Inside the Ruins*, Rootsy/Warner Music, 2008.

Måndotter, Lena & Skin to Skin, *Walking on Water*, Chameleon Records, 2002.

Måndotter, Lena & Skin to Skin, *Temenos*, Waveform Records, 2002.

Måndotter, Lena & Skin to Skin, *In the Shadow of Love*, S2S Records, 1999.

Måndotter, Lena & Magna, *Nordic Chants*, S2S Records, 1999.

Måndotter, Lena & Skin to Skin, *Live Acoustic*, Chameleon Records, 1998.

Måndotter, Lena, *Letters to a Young Singer* (film on song and psyche), Kameleont Production, 2009.

Måndotter, Lena, *Sierskans Brev*, (The Seeress' Letter), Kameleont Production, 2016.

Måndotter, Lena, *I Min Grekiska By*, (In My Greek Village), Kameleont Production, 2004.

Måndotter, Lena, *Där Alla Änglar Fallit*, (Where All Angels Have Fallen), a journey in Tibet to the holy mountain Kailash). Art Distribution, 1992.

Måndotter, Lena & Törnlund, Niklas, *Asien – Mystik och Verklighet*, (Asia – Mystery and Reality), FC Syd, 1994.

Måndotter, Lena, *Offra Denna Dröm* (Sacrifice this Dream) – a lyrical travel diary from Mexico and Guatemala, Art Distribution, 1991.

Neumann, Eric, *The Great Mother – an Analysis of an Archetype,* Princeton University Press, 1972.

Neumann, Eric, *Art and the Creative Unconscious*, Princeton University Press, 1974.

Newham, Paul, *The Singing Cure – an Introduction to Voice Movement Therapy*, Shambhala Publications, 1994.

Newham, Paul, *The Prophet of Song – the Life and Work of Alfred Wolfsohn*, Tigers Eye Press, 1997.

Newham, Paul, *Therapeutic Voicework – Principles and Practice for the Use of Singing as a Therapy*, Jessica Kingsley Publishers, 1998.

Newham, Paul, *Using Voice and Song in Therapy – The Practical Application of Voice Movement Therapy*, Jessica Kingsley Publishers, 1999.

Otto, Rudolf, *The Idea of the Holy – an Inquiry into the Non-rational in the Idea of the Divine and its Relation to the Rational*, Penguin Books, 1959.

Otto, Walter F.,*The Homeric Gods – the Spiritual Significance of Greek Religion*, Thames and Hudson, 1979.

Pena-Guzman, David, *When Animals Dream – The Hidden World of Animal Consciousness*, Princeton University Press, 2022.

Pétrement, Simone, *Simon Weil: A Life*, Pantheon Books, 1976.

Pinkola Estés, Clarissa, *Women Who Run with the Wolves*, Rider/Random House, 1998.

Radin, Paul, *The Trickster: a Study in American Indian Mythology*, Schocken Books, 1972.

Raine, Kathleen, *W B Yeats and the Learning of the Imagination*, Golgonooza Press, 1999.

Raine, Kathleen, *The Inner Journey of the Poet*, ed. Brian Keeble, George Allen & Unwin, 1982.

Ralston Saul, John, *Voltaire's Bastards: The Dictatorship of Reason in the West,* Simon & Schuster, 1992.

Reeves, Paula M., *Heart Sense: Unlocking Your Highest Purpose and Deepest Desires,* Conari Press, 2003.

Richards, Thomas, *At Work with Grotowski*, Routledge, 1995.

Russack, Neil, *Animal Guides in Life, Myth and Dream*, Inner City Books, 2002.

Salvatore, Gianfranco, *Orpheus before Orpheus*, essay in Spring Journal *Orpheus*, vol 71, 2004.

Scholem, Gershom, *On the Kabbalah and its Symbolism*, Schocken Books, 1996.

Schweizer, Andreas, *The Sungod's Journey through the Netherworld*, Cornell University Press, 2010.

Simmons, Sylvie, *I'm Your Man – the Life of Leonard Cohen*, Vintage Books, 2013.

Skar, Patricia, *The Matrix of Music and Analysis*, in anthology *Music and Psyche*, ed. P. Ashton and S. Bloch, Spring Journal Books, 2010.

Stein, Murray, *In Midlife – a Jungian Perspective*, Spring Publications, 2009.

Stein, Murray, *The Principle of Individuation*, Chiron Publications, 2006.

Stein, Murray, *Jung's Map of the Soul*, Open Court/Carus Publ., 2010.

Tarkovky, Andrey, *Sculpting in Time – Reflections on the Cinema*, Texas University Press, 2010, transl. Kitty Hunter-Blair.

Taylor, Anne Elizabeth, *Unveiling Sophia – Heart Wisdom in an Age of Technology*, Chiron Publications, 2021.

Tiberghien, Susan M., *Writing Towards Wholeness – Lessons Inspired by C.G. Jung*, Chiron Publications, 2018.

Tomatis, Alfred, *The Conscious Ear: My Life of Transformation Through Listening,* Station Hill Press, 1991.

Ueland, Brenda, *If You Want to Write – a book about Art, Independence and Spirit*, Graywolf Press, 1987, Origin. Putnam 1938.

Uzdavinys, Algis, *Orpheus and the Roots of Platonism*, The Matheson Trust, 2011.

Vaughan-Lee, Llewellyn, *Prayer of the Heart in Christian & Sufi Mysticism*, Golden Sufi Center, 2017.

Von Franz, Marie-Louise, *Time – Rhythm and Repose*, Thames & Hudson, 1978, reprint 1992.

Von Franz, Marie-Louise, *Shadow and Evil in Fairytales*, Shambhala Publ., 1995.

Von Franz, Marie-Louise, *Projection and Re-collection in Jungian Psychology: Reflections of the Soul*, Open Court Publ.,1995.

Von Franz, Marie-Louise, *Archetypal Dimensions of the Psyche*, Shambhala Publications, 1999.

Von Franz, Marie-Louise, *Numbers and Time: Reflections Leading Toward a Unification of Depth Psychology and Physics*, Northwestern University Press, 1974.

Von Franz, Marie-Louise, *Psychotherapy*, Shambhala Publications, 1993.

Von Franz, Marie-Louise, *Psyche and Matter*, Shambhala Publications, 1982.

Von Franz, Marie-Louise, *The Cat – a Tale of Feminine Redemption*, Inner City Books, 1999.

Weil, Simone, *Waiting for God*, Harper and Row, 1973.

Wilkinson, Margaret, *Coming Into Mind*, Routledge, 2009.

Wolfsohn, Alfred, *Orpheus or the Way to a Mask*, Abraxas Publishing, 2012.

Woloy, Eleanora, *The Symbol of the Dog in the Human Psyche*, Chiron Publications, 1990.

Woodman, Marion, *The Owl was a Baker's Daughter (Obesity, Anorexia Nervosa and the Repressed Feminine),* Inner City Books, 1980.

Woodman, Marion, *Addiction to Perfection (The Still Unravished Bride),* Inner City Books, 1982.

Woodman, Marion, *The Pregnant Virgin (A Process of Psychological Transformation),* Inner City Books, 1985.

Woodman, Marion, *The Ravaged Bridegroom (Masculinity in Women),* Inner City Books, 1990.

Woodman, Marion, *Conscious Femininity (Interviews with Marion Woodman),* Inner City Books, 1993.

Woodman, Marion and Elinor Dickson, *Dancing in the Flames (The Dark Goddess in the Transformation of Consciousness),* Gill & Macmillan, 1996.

Wroe, Ann, *Orpheus – the Song of Life*, Pimlico, 2012.

Zuckerkandl, Victor, *Man the Musician*, Princeton University Press, Bollingen Series, transl. Norbert Guterman, 1976.

Zuckerkandl, Victor, *Sound and Symbol – Music and the Eternal World*, Princeton University Press, Bollingen Foundation, 1973. (orig. 1956)

Zuckerkandl, Victor, *The Sense of Music*, Princeton University Press, 1971. (orig. 1959)

Journals/Yearbooks/Bibles/Lexicon

The Holy Bible, King James Version

The Mysteries – Papers from the Eranos Yearbooks, ed. Joseph Campbell, Bollingen Series XXX Vol. 2, Princeton University Press, 1990.

Color Symbolism, The Eranos Lectures, ed. Klaus Ottmann, Spring Publications, 2005.

Spring – a Journal of Archetype and Culture, Vol. 83, *Minding the Animal Psyche*, ed. N. Cater and G. A. Bradshaw, 2010.

Spring – a Journal of Archetype and Culture, Vol. 82, *The Symbolic Life*, ed. N. Cater/M. Stein, 2009.

Spring – a Journal of Archetype and Culture, Vol. 71, *Orpheus*, ed. N. Cater, 2004.

Elsevier's Dictionary of Symbols and Imagery, ed. Ad De Vries, Elsevier, 2009.

Encyclopaedia of Archetypal Symbolism, ed. Beverly Moon, Shambala, 1991.

Encyclopaedia of Religion & Ethics Volume XI, ed. J. Hastings, T&T Ltd., 1920.

Penguins Dictionary of Symbols, London, 1996.

The Book of Symbols – Reflections on Archetypal Images, Taschen, 2010.

LECTURES/SEMINARS/SUPERVISION

Egger, Brigitte, seminar series on *Synchronicity*, ISAP Zürich, 2011.

Jacoby, Mario, lecture series *The Wounded Healer* at C.G. Jung Institut, Küsnacht Zürich, 2000. and at ISAP – International School of Analytical Psychology Zürich, 2010.

Jacoby, Mario, supervision sessions in song-therapy, Zürich, 2010/2011.

Newham, Paul, lecture *Voice Movement Therapy*, London, 1997.

Romare, Ingela, seminars on *the films of Andrey Tarkovsky*, Malmö/Sweden. 1998/1999.

Woodman, Marion, *BodySoul Rhythms* training, Einsiedeln, Switzerland, 2008/2009.

AUTHOR BIOGRAPHY

Photo by Thomas Frantzén

Lena Måndotter is a singer/song-therapist (dipl. RSA - The Royal Society of Arts, London, IAVMT) and a Jungian psychoanalyst (dipl. ISAP - The International School of Analytical Psychology, Zürich, AGAP/IAAP).

For the last 30 years Lena has given courses, seminars and individual sessions in song-therapy and the healing power of creativity.

She is a regular teacher at ISAP – The International School of Analytical Psychology in Zürich. The focus of her work is the transpersonal dimension of sound and psyche, song and soul. She has also taught at The Royal College of Music in Stockholm, Malmö University and for many Jungian organizations and other centers and companies.

Besides her Jungian psychoanalytic and song-therapeutic trainings Lena has also done extensive studies with internationally known writer and Jungian analyst Marion Woodman and her BodySoul Rhythms courses. To deepen her knowledge in creativity she has studied literature and poetry at Lund's University in Sweden and other studies in music, photography, film, art, and performance.

Lena's film, "Letters to a Young Singer," a journey into the mythological world of song and soul, was filmed in the Cretan mountains of Greece, where she lived for many years. The film had its premiere at one of

Sweden's biggest film-festivals and has then been shown at various venues, festivals and international seminars.

Besides her therapeutic work Lena has been involved in many creative projects within the world of music, poetry, painting, and photography. Many of her performances and audio-visual installations have been shown at Malmö Konsthall, one of Northern Europe's largest exhibition spaces of contemporary art. She has published several books of poetry and about travels she has made to Tibet, Ladakh, Nepal, Burma, India, Mexico, Guatemala, and Greece.

She has given photographic exhibitions and released a series of music-albums and toured nationally and internationally since 1990. Her creative work has been awarded many grants and funding from well-known cultural institutions and during her long artistic carrier both media and audience have given a warm response.

For more information about Lena Måndotter's artistic, psychoanalytic, and song-therapeutic work: www.lenamandotter.com

ACKNOWLEDGEMENTS

I am profoundly grateful for the love and unwavering belief in my creative work which has been given to me during all these years by my husband and musical companion Ronnie Hall.

My friends' and audiences' warm support of my creative path has been so important, and my co-musicians and many other musical beings inspire me deeply. I am also very grateful for my friend Lisa Forstenius' precious help given to this specific book project.

My dogs, on this and the other side of the rainbow, I will always honor you and your profound wisdom and loving presence.

For making many artistic, musical, Jungian and song-therapeutic projects possible during all these years, I give my heartful thanks to all donors and funders and, on my website, I list you all.

There are so many soul guides that I have met in my life and for your wise guidance I bow down humbly. I also give thanks to all my students and clients for being such good teachers of song and of soul.

And then, of course, nothing musical could have been accomplished without Hermes, Orpheus and all the other Divine Beings of the Imaginal Realm.

There is so much more to be grateful for and so many more to tell it to, so here I can just bow, with hands together, palm to palm, and sing in praise to the invisible ones and to the sounding One.

And, finally, but not least, I feel deep gratitude to my editor Jennifer Fitzgerald and to Murray Stein and Chiron Publications for believing in me as a writer and releasing this book *The Song of the Soul* and inviting me to sing and give lectures at the *Zürich Lecture Series* 2024.

Index

www.ingramcontent.com/pod-product-compliance
Lightning Source LLC
Chambersburg PA
CBHW020705270326
41928CB00005B/275